The Choice

A Fable of Free Trade and Protectionism

The Choice

A Fable of Free Trade and Protectionism

Third Edition

Russell Roberts

George Mason University

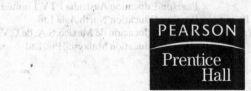

PEARSON

Prentice Hall

Upper Saddle River, New Jersey 07458

To my parents, Ted and Shirley Roberts, who taught me to love words, life, and the world

Library of Congress Cataloging-in-Publication Data

Roberts, Russell D.
    The choice : a fable of free trade and protectionism / Russell D. Roberts.—3rd ed.
      p. cm.
    Includes index.
    ISBN 0-13-143354-7
    1. Free trade.   2. Protectionism.   3. Free trade—United States.   4. Protectionism—
United States.   5. Ricardo, David, 1772–1823.   I. Title.
HF1713.R615 2007
330.12'2—dc22

                         2006025248

Editor: Jon Axelrod
VP/Editorial Director: Jeff Shelstad
Editorial Assistant: Michael Dittamo
Assistant Editor: Mary Kate Murray
AVP/ Executive Marketing Manager: Sharon Koch
Marketing Assistant: Patrick Barbera
Managing Editor (Production): Cynthia Zonneveld
Production Editor: Melissa Feimer
Permissions Supervisor: Charles Morris
Manufacturing Buyer: Michelle Klein
Cover Photo: Hulton Archive/Taxi/Getty Images
Composition/Full-Service Project Management: Stratford Publishing Services

---

Pearson Education LTD.   Pearson Education Australia PTY, Limited
Pearson Education Singapore, Pte. Ltd   Pearson Education North Asia Ltd
Pearson Education, Canada, Ltd   Pearson Educación de Mexico, S.A. de C.V.
Pearson Education–Japan   Pearson Education Malaysia, Pte. Ltd

ISBN 0-13-143354-7

Preface to the Third Edition

The first edition of this book was written in the early 1990s, when Americans were worried about the threat of Japan to our standard of living. The second edition was written after the passage of NAFTA, when Americans were worried that Mexico was a threat to our standard of living. Both of those threats and the fears they created turned out to be short lived. I believe that current fears about China and India's threat to our standard of living will turn out the same way.

I have updated this edition to discuss the growing economic strength of China and India. Just as worries about trade with Japan and Mexico turned out to be grossly inaccurate, I do not believe that China and India pose any economic threat to America. In fact, the opposite is true. Trade with China and India is good for most Americans. Trade with China and India makes America a richer country in both the financial sense and in the sense of expanded opportunity to live a meaningful life.

In addition to updating the numbers to 2005 where possible, this new edition adds chapters on the role of manufacturing jobs in our economy, the economic effects of outsourcing, and the role of the World Bank and the International Monetary Fund in fighting global poverty. I have also tried to improve the discussion of comparative advantage and moved material to where I thought it made the most sense.

Russell Roberts (roberts@gmu.edu)
George Mason University
Fairfax, Virginia
May 2006

Acknowledgments

The Talmud says, "I have learned much from my teachers, more from my colleagues, and most of all from my students" (Taanis 7a). My general interest in trade began with Milton Friedman's *Capitalism and Freedom* and continued during my undergraduate years at the University of North Carolina with a course from James Ingram. His book *International Economic Problems* uses a metaphor of an import/export business as a factory that helped inspire my approach here.

In graduate school at the University of Chicago, I was fortunate to learn about trade issues in my microeconomics class from D. McCloskey. The diagrams and intuition from that class greatly influenced my teaching and thinking. I have taught that analysis to thousands of students while teaching at the University of Rochester, Stanford University, UCLA, Washington University in St. Louis, and George Mason University. Many of the questions asked by those students have found their way to the mouth of Ed Johnson. I am grateful to my students for their passion, questions, and interest.

George Stigler gave me an enormous dose of skepticism about industry statements on their motives for supporting government legislation. I am sorry he did not live to see this book. I would have loved to chat with him about David Ricardo.

I'm grateful to Jon Axelrod of Prentice Hall for pushing me to do a third edition. I wish to thank Howard Swaine and Dan Stastny for finding mistakes or sources of confusion in the previous edition. Michael Cardwell did a superb job on the research to bring the numbers up to date for this new edition. Any errors are my own. I want to thank Virginia Postrel for the insight that not all jobs in America end up in Mississippi or Arkansas just because wages are low there.

I particularly want to thank my colleague Don Boudreaux for hours of conversation on comparative advantage, outsourcing, and the trade deficit. I have learned an immense amount from Don, and much of that knowledge is in these pages.

I thank Menlo Smith for guidance and support.

I wish to thank Dan Gressel, Kent Kimbrough, John Lott Jr., and Richard McKenzie for many helpful conversations about trade issues.

I had helpful conversations with Eric Schuster of Motorola; Simon Bonita, Takehiko Hayakawa, and Noel Howard of Merck; and Hendrik Verfaille and Scott Koehne of Monsanto about their companies.

I want to thank Steve Goodman for insights into retailing and Zev Fredman for continued scholarship on Frank Sinatra, which came in handy.

I am grateful to Stephen Dietrich for his faith and efforts as editor of the first edition of this book and Sally Denlow for her boundless energy and enthusiasm, especially in the early going, which made all the difference. I thank Rod Banister of Prentice Hall for his encouragement and help with the second edition. I am grateful for suggestions provided by the following reviewers: Allen R. Sanderson at the University of Chicago, Thomas Mitchell at Southern Illinois University, Steven Suranovic at George Washington University, Peter Mueser at the University of Missouri–Columbia, Joseph P. McGarrity at the University of Central Arkansas, Anthony J. Guglielmi at the University of Massachusetts–Amherst, Matthew Brown at Santa Clara University, Jonathan Crystal at Fordham University, Michael A. McPherson at University of North Texas, Farhad Rassekh at the University of Hartford, and especially Michael McElroy of North Carolina State University.

Thomas Egan, Rob Freund, Catherine Bradford, and Marc Law provided research support for earlier editions.

Friends, family, and colleagues gave me support and many helpful suggestions for improving the earlier editions. I wish to thank Andy Akin, Marci Armstrong, Catherine Bradford, Denise Dill, Jennifer Chilton, Steve Goodman, Ron Jones, Suki Kotler, Marc Law, Michael Levin, Pat Masidonski, Gary Miller, Stephen Moss, Lisa and Randy Harris, Joe and Jennifer Roberts, Gregg Rotenberg, Phyllis Shapiro, Murray Weidenbaum, and Michael Wolkoff for their help. I wish to thank Alan Deardorff of the University of Michigan, Don Schilling at the University of Missouri, Pat Welch at St. Louis University, and Judy Ware of Crossroads School, along with their students, who used early versions of the manuscript and gave me many helpful comments.

Special thanks go to Don Boudeaux, Zev Fredman, Bevis Schock, and my parents, Shirley and Ted Roberts, for reading early versions of the manuscript multiple times and providing excellent feedback at every turn.

I want to thank my wife, Sharon, for her innumerable comments on innumerable drafts, her unflagging support, and her patience with my hours at the computer. She has been a perpetual sounding board for the ideas I have tried to capture here. Any success this book has would be meaningless without her.

When I wrote the first edition of this book, my wife and I had one child. We have now been blessed with four children. I hope they inherit a world with the opportunities for expression and wonder that would make David Ricardo proud.

Contents

DAVID RICARDO

English economist, widely regarded as one of the greatest practitioners of the deductive method of analysis in economics. He was born in London on April 18, 1772, to orthodox Jewish parents and studied from the age of 11 to 13 at the Talmud Torah attached to the Portuguese Synagogue in Amsterdam. Ricardo became estranged from his family when he became a Unitarian and married a Quaker in 1793. He was first employed by his father in the London Stock Exchange in 1786 and operated there independently from 1793 to 1816. By 1813, he had amassed a large fortune and retired from business. He served in the House of Commons as the member from Portarlington from 1819 until his death in Gloucestershire on September 11, 1823. Ricardo's most famous work, *On the Principles of Political Economy and Taxation*, first appeared in 1817.

from the *Encyclopedia Americana*

George Marks/Getty Images Inc – Retrofile Royalty Free

ED JOHNSON

Ed Johnson was born in 1917 in Star, Illinois. He received a degree in engineering from the University of Illinois in 1939. Johnson served in the U.S. Army during World War II, achieving the rank of major. He earned a Silver Star for gallantry in action at Omaha Beach in the D-Day operation. After the war, he returned to Star to work in the Stellar Television Company. He was named president of the company in 1955. He married Martha Hellman in 1948. The Johnsons had two children, Steven and Susan.

Author's Note

The Stellar Television Company; Star, Illinois, and its citizens; and Congressman Frank Bates are products of the author's imagination. Any resemblance of these characters to any persons, living or dead, is purely coincidental. All of the other companies and people are real. I have tried to portray them and the American economy as accurately as possible. Sources are found at the conclusion of the story, in Chapter 17.

CHAPTER

Minutes of the Heavenly Court: Soul of David Ricardo

INITIAL TRIAL

DATE: September 11, 1823

MAGISTRATE: Please state pertinent biographical detail.

DEFENDANT: I was born in 1772 and given the name David Ricardo. My mother, peace be upon her, named me after King David, writer of psalms, sweet singer of Israel. She—

MAGISTRATE: Mr. Ricardo. Less lyricism. More facts. Occupation?

DEFENDANT: I was chiefly a financier, then later a politician.

MAGISTRATE: Speak up, Mr. Ricardo. Your occupation will not be held against you. What do you consider your most important achievement while you were alive?

DEFENDANT: My theory of comparative advantage. Outlined in my 1817 book, *On the Principles of Political Economy and Taxation,* the theory showed how nations benefit from free trade. In addition, as a member of the British Parliament, I spoke numerous times on the dangers of protectionism and the benefits of free trade.

MAGISTRATE: Were your views heeded?

DEFENDANT: Not yet, but in time I believe—

MAGISTRATE: That will be all, Mr. Ricardo. You are sentenced to a period of wandering until further evidence is brought to the attention of this court.

REQUEST FOR RETRIAL

DATE: December 18, 1846

MAGISTRATE: Mr. Ricardo. You have requested this hearing to put forward additional evidence you believe relevant to your case.

DEFENDANT: Yes. I am happy to report that down below, my native country of England has abolished the Corn Laws that protected British farmers from foreign competition. I request that the court consider reopening my case.

MAGISTRATE: Request dismissed. It is too early to tell if this change is temporary or permanent. In addition, do not virtually

1

all nations outside of Britain still practice extensive trade restrictions?

DEFENDANT: Yes, but—

MAGISTRATE: That will be all, Mr. Ricardo.

REQUEST FOR TOUCHING DOWN

DATE: July 13, 1960

MAGISTRATE: Mr. Ricardo. You have requested an opportunity to intervene in human affairs to remove your status as a wanderer. What evidence justifies your request?

DEFENDANT: I believe the United States is about to embark on a policy of protectionism that will destroy the American economy. I request one evening on Earth to help put America on the path of freer trade and prosperity.

MAGISTRATE: Request granted. You realize, Mr. Ricardo, that a wanderer is allowed only one period of touching down during the probationary period.

DEFENDANT: Yes, sir. I feel confident that—

MAGISTRATE: That will be all, Mr. Ricardo. Good luck. And Godspeed.

CHAPTER 2

The Challenge of Foreign Competition

"When our factory opened, a worker made $50 per week, and over at Willie's Appliance Store, a Stellar television cost $250. So it took a worker five weeks of work to earn a television. Today, the average worker in that factory makes $100 per week and Willie gets $200 for a Stellar television—two weeks of work to earn a television. That's how I measure our success—how many hours it takes one of you to earn one of our products. That number has been falling since the first year of operation."

That was Ed Johnson talking back in 1959, a year before I touched down. Ed's the chief executive officer of Stellar Television Company. Their headquarters are in Star, Illinois, the destination for my one night back on Earth. If you had been dead for 137 years and had one evening back on Earth, you probably wouldn't head for a town of 100,000 people in Illinois. But Ed Johnson and Star hold the key to my future and America's. I thought you'd like to get to know Ed and his company before I touched down.

Ed was speaking at the annual company picnic, held every year in Johnson Park. They named the park for his father, who started the company. Ed always has a great time. He brings the family, tears his pants sliding into second in the softball game, and eats a lot of fried chicken and potato salad. Ed gets along fine with the workers—he worked in the factory in high school before heading off to study engineering. Stellar has three other factories around the state, but the one in Star's the biggest. In a good month, the 5,000 workers in Star make 80,000 televisions.

As you can tell from Ed's speech, Ed is pretty proud of his company. But walking home from the picnic, his wife Martha sensed something was wrong. She waited until their two children ran up ahead and out of earshot.

"What's bothering you, dear?"

"Foreign competition. Japanese televisions are coming into America. I almost had to lay off workers this month. And I may have to lower wages and break the streak I talked about this afternoon."

"Oh, honey, you're teasing. People know that 'Made in Japan' means junk. No one is going to buy a Japanese television."

"Some are buying them now."

3

The next morning, after a restless night, Ed drove into Chicago and took a plane to Washington. He met with his congressman, Frank Bates. He asked for a limit on imports of Japanese televisions. Eliminating foreign competition would keep the jobs and wages of his workers safe.

"Well now, Ed, I just don't know. You've been good to me, always helping out with the campaign, and I appreciate that. But this kind of bill is tricky. People want a level playing field. Competition is the American way of life. Playing tough with the Japanese isn't going to look good."

"That's nonsense, Frank. We invented the television. The Japanese stole it from us. Now they're stealing our jobs. If good jobs go to Japan, what will we replace them with? What will happen to Star? And what will happen to the companies around Chicago that supply us? If Stellar Television closes, the trouble doesn't end in Star, it just begins there! We can't let the Japanese get ahead. They'll get all the future inventions in electronics if our television industry disappears."

"I hear what you're saying, Ed. Hey, I fought in the Pacific. Listen, Ed. There's serious talk of me making a real run at the White House. I don't need some trade bill around my neck. Let me get in the White House, and then I can help."

"How are you going to run for president if people in your home district are having trouble making ends meet? A bill like this can put you in the White House. You just have to explain it right. Buying American will make America rich again."

"It sounds better when you put it that way. Let me think it over."

Frank Bates thought it over and decided to sponsor a bill banning foreign televisions. Every month another 80,000 televisions came off the line at Stellar Television, and every month there was more talk of Congressman Bates becoming President Bates someday. His trade bill banning imports of televisions passed. He started speaking about a plan to keep out all foreign products entirely, to pass on the benefits to other industries, not just televisions. That plan became the centerpiece of his presidential campaign. Ed Johnson did a lot of traveling and speaking for Frank Bates, defending protectionism.

By the summer of 1960, Frank Bates was even money to get his party's nomination. He asked Ed to make one of his nominating speeches at the convention. Ed hesitated, but Frank explained that his staff would write the speech for him. Ed would talk about the glory of America and the importance of protecting basic American industries from foreign competition. He'd explain how Frank's economic policies would lead to prosperity for all, just as it had for Stellar's workers and the citizens of Star. It didn't seem too difficult. Ed said yes.

The night before his plane was due to leave for the convention in Los Angeles, Ed Johnson tossed and turned in bed, unable to sleep. He had practiced his speech. His wife and kids were healthy and asleep on a July night in Illinois. His workers had never fared better. Stellar televisions were selling for $300, but his workers earned up to $200 a week, working only a week and a half to earn a television. The plant was at full capacity, and there had been talk of expanding. What was bothering Ed Johnson?

At 2:00 A.M. Ed headed downstairs for a glass of milk and a piece of chocolate cake. He went back upstairs to the den, talking to himself. He walked over to the hi-fi, put on Frank Sinatra's *Only the Lonely,* and placed the needle on the mournful "One for My Baby."

"Never did like government," he muttered. "I admit that quota bill sure has been good for Stellar Television. But I'm worried about a bill that would limit all foreign imports. Televisions are different. Electronics are the future of America. But all products? Maybe it won't turn out so well."

That was my cue. So while Ed was pacing the room, I got the Magistrate to approve my request to come back to Earth for a night. Then I popped into the leather armchair in the corner. Ed didn't see me at first; he was too busy digging a trench in the carpet. When I finally caught his eye, he came to a full stop and gave out a snort of breath. His words of greeting were a nervous staccato.

"Whoa, my friend, who the hell are you?"

I had not heard much profanity from Ed Johnson in all the years I had observed him. Arriving unannounced in a man's den at two in the morning will jar even the most peaceful spirit.

"My name is David, but you can call me Dave. I'm—"

"Look here, Dave," said Ed gently, "are you hungry? There's fried chicken downstairs. How about a piece?"

Ed had taken me for a beggar of some kind, looking for a warm place to stay and a meal. No call to the authorities. Just an offer of help.

"Thank you kindly, Mr. Johnson. I wish I could accept your offer, I truly do. Where I come from, we don't get hungry."

"Plenty to eat where you come from, then?" asked Ed in a nervous voice. The temperature had fallen in the room and Ed began checking the windows while he was talking, looking for a draft.

"The windows are all fine, Mr. Johnson. That draft you're feeling is my doing, I'm afraid. It's a natural consequence when a wanderer touches down."

"A wanderer?"

"Yes. Mr. Johnson, have you ever seen *It's a Wonderful Life?*"

"Of course. See it every Christmas. One of my favorite movies."

"You remember Clarence in that film?"

"Sure. Clarence was George Bailey's guardian angel. Great how he got his wings in the end. Now, Dave, let's head downstairs. I'm sure there's something in the icebox to interest you."

"I'm afraid it doesn't quite work that way."

"What doesn't work what way?"

"Getting the wings. Mr. Capra was merely being fanciful."

"Is that so?" Ed reached for the telephone on his desk. "Why won't this phone work?" Ed asked, speaking to himself.

"Probably my doing, though I daresay I can't explain it. More in your line of work, I would venture. Electricity, televisions—"

"Listen, Mr. David whatever-your-last-name-is—"

"Ricardo."

"Listen, Mr. Ricardo, if you've cut my phone line, I am going to lose my sense of humor—"

"Calm down, Mr. Johnson. Remember in *It's a Wonderful Life* how Clarence proves he's an angel? I just have to do something similar for you."

"Why don't you tell me why I'm eating milk and chocolate cake?"

"Not too difficult. When you were a boy, you used to go downstairs with your father on the pretext of making sure the lights were out. He would give you a glass of milk and a piece of chocolate cake. You and Steven have continued the ritual, but tonight, it is too late for Steven."

Ed sat down. I'd gotten his attention.

"Parlor tricks are so demeaning, Ed. May I call you Ed? I know you very well, far better than one who would know about the scar on your knee from that nasty fall as a child. Such knowledge does not establish my unearthly origins—a man with enough nerve and gumption could uncover such a detail. No, Ed, my ear is more finely tuned than you can imagine. I know of your dreams for your son Steven and how you yearn to see your daughter Susan safe and secure. I, too, had such dreams for my children. I know your uneasiness at the thought of your alliance with Mr. Bates. You tossed and turned in bed tonight because of guilt, wasn't it? Guilt at knowing you had turned to others for help, that you sought unfair advantage for your company . . . ."

Ed Johnson's gaze had softened, and I knew I had struck home.

"Patience, Ed. You'll have real cause for guilt before the night is through. But you will have a chance for redemption that few men are given."

"I am at your service."

"We are going to travel in time. I am going to show you what will become of America if Frank Bates fails in his bid for the presidency. If Frank Bates becomes president of the United States, America will become increasingly protectionist. Instead, I am going to show you the America of increasingly free trade. Perhaps when you see such a world, you will no longer support Frank Bates, and you will throw away that speech on your night table."

"I'm ready, Mr. Ricardo."

"Call me Dave."

"You don't have relatives in Cuba by any chance?"

"Cuba? I don't think so. Most of my relatives remain in England."

"The phrase 'Babaloo' doesn't mean anything to you, then?"

"Ah, I catch the allusion. Very good, Ed. But I am afraid that is another Ricardo. No relation."

On that note, we soared into the future.

CHAPTER

The Roundabout
Way to Wealth

I chose the year 2005 to play it safe. That would give Ed enough of a taste of a world where Americans were free to trade with foreigners.

"Where are we?" asked Ed.

"My friend, we are in the parking lot of a movie theater in your hometown of Star, Illinois, in the year 2005."

"Why would a movie theater need such a large parking lot?"

"There are 16 theaters here, and they need a lot of space."

"Sixteen theaters! What happened to the Bijou?"

"The Bijou, downtown? I'm afraid it was torn down in the name of something called 'urban renewal.' "

"That's too bad. Can we see the Stellar Television factory?"

"I'm afraid it's gone, Ed."

"Gone!" cried Ed, leaning against a Honda Accord for emotional support.

"I'm afraid so. In fact, this multiplex—the modern name for a collection of theaters—stands on the very spot where your plant once stood."

"I'll be damned, why—"

"Ed, watch your language. You may get your wish."

"Sorry. Is anyone making televisions in the United States anymore?"

"They are. In fact, they're doing it with lower labor and raw material costs than you did in your best year."

"Must be Motorola. They always gave me a good fight."

"Motorola made its last television in 1974."

"Then who is it?"

"I'll show you. We'll have to leave Star for a bit. But that shouldn't be any problem for the people Upstairs."

"Where are we now, Dave?"

"Rahway, New Jersey."

"Where's the television factory?"

"You're looking at it."

"But the sign says 'Merck and Co., Inc., A Pharmaceutical Company.' Doesn't that mean they make drugs?"

"Indeed they do, Ed. They send some of those drugs to Japan. In return, Japan sends America televisions. There are two ways to make a television set—the direct way, and the roundabout way. The direct way is to build a factory like yours in Star and combine raw materials with people and machines to produce televisions. With the roundabout way of making televisions, you make televisions by making something else, such as drugs, and trading the drugs for televisions. Japan's drug industry isn't able to efficiently create and supply all of Japan's demand for drugs, so Japan imports drugs and exports televisions. What you see appears to be a drug manufacturer. But they also produce televisions for Americans to enjoy by exporting some of their production."

"But Merck doesn't send drugs to Japan for televisions. They send drugs to Japan for money."

"That is how matters appear. But Merck accepts Japanese currency for their drugs only because some American wants to use that currency to buy something from Japan such as televisions. If no one wanted to buy Japanese products, then Merck would have to use that currency as wallpaper. They wouldn't sell drugs to Japan."

"Couldn't they exchange the yen for dollars at a bank?"

"They can, as matters turn out. But matters turn out that way only because someone with dollars wants to buy something made in Japan and needs yen to do it. Otherwise, no one would give up dollars for yen, and the bank would not be in the business of currency exchange. You see Americans buying televisions and giving the Japanese dollars. And Japanese buying drugs with yen. But actually, Americans are swapping drugs for televisions. The currencies merely facilitate the transaction."

Ed looked at me warily.

"What happens when Japan increases its supply of domestically produced drugs?"

"Maybe they will, or maybe they won't. Japan can't make everything. Well, they can, but they can't make everything equally well. Like every nation, their resources are limited. By their resources, I don't mean just raw materials; I mean their people, and the number of hours in a day, and how hard people wish to work. It's impossible for Japan to make everything better than anyone else in the world. And even if they could, it wouldn't be wise for them to do so."

"Why not?"

"Even if they could, they would do even better by specializing in a few things rather than trying to do everything. Take yourself. I know you won the typing contest at Star High your senior year. Set the all-time record, didn't you?"

"I did."

"Yet as president of Stellar Television, don't you have your own secretary?"

"Of course."

"But you are a better typist than she is. Why did you hire her?"

"Because my time is better spent running the plant."

"Exactly. Your time is scarce. So even though you type much more quickly than Miss Evers, it would be foolish for you to do the typing. The same is true of Japan. As a nation, they specialize in producing televisions and import drugs even though they could train their television engineers to be chemists. America, in turn, wants both life-saving drugs and televisions. It produces both in the most efficient way possible: by making drugs, keeping some for domestic consumption, and sending the rest to Japan for televisions."

"Does this insight have a name?"

"It does, but it is not so catchy: 'The Theory of Comparative Advantage.' A British economist figured it out."

"Who was that economist, Dave?"

"I cannot say I remember, Ed. At any rate, you and I will give it a different name: 'The Roundabout Way to Wealth.' The idea is that even if a nation is relatively poor at doing everything, there are some things it does relatively well. And a nation that is really good at many things should still specialize in producing some items and import the rest."

"I don't understand."

"Neither do most students. A numerical example might help, but it also might put you to sleep, and we have a long night ahead of us. And that numerical example leads some students to think that the theory applies only when there are two goods or two countries in the world. Let me try to cut to the essence of it. Time is the ultimate scarce resource. You should use your time wisely. Trying to do everything for yourself is actually expensive—it means taking time away from those things you do relatively well. So you hire Miss Evers to do your typing, even though you're a better typist than she is. The same is true for nations. Even though the United States excels at television production, devoting scarce resources to televisions means having less of something else. So as good as Americans are at making televisions, Americans are even better at making pharmaceuticals. The United States has a comparative advantage in pharmaceuticals, even though it might take less labor to produce a television in the United States than it does in Japan."

"But, Ed. If it takes less labor to produce a television in the United States than it does in Japan, isn't it inefficient to have the Japanese make televisions instead of Americans?"

"No, because people don't care just about televisions. They care about other things as well. The real cost of making televisions in America isn't the labor that is devoted to the task but rather what that labor could have produced instead. Making televisions means making less of something else. Suppose America is a little better than Japan at making televisions, but a lot better at making pharmaceuticals. Then making televisions in America is expensive—it means giving up a lot of pharmaceutical production.

Better to let the Japanese make televisions, just like you gave up typing to concentrate on managing your factory. Or maybe a better way to say it is like this—better to make lots of pharmaceuticals and use some of them to make televisions the roundabout way—by swapping some of them for televisions. That way you get more televisions than you would have by trying to make them directly."

"And I guess Japan is doing the same thing. They're getting richer by making televisions and swapping them for drugs rather than trying to make drugs for themselves."

"That's right. The whole idea of trading with another nation is the same idea as trading with people in your own country. It's a way to let people use their skills together. Trade looks like competition. But it's really a form of cooperation. Japan makes televisions for Americans, and in return Americans make pharmaceuticals for the Japanese. By trading with others, you leverage your skills in a way you could never do if you tried to do everything for yourself. Trade is the way to get the most out of your skills and your scarce time—for both sides of the deal."

"But how do you know the roundabout way is cheaper? It's just a theory. The government stands back and lets Motorola and Stellar go out of business—"

"Motorola is still in business, Ed."

"But you said—"

"I said they stopped making televisions."

"OK, they stopped making televisions. So America makes televisions in the roundabout way. But Americans are sending money to Japan. Lots of money, I bet. Wouldn't it be better for the United States if that money stayed in America? That way, Americans have the money instead of the Japanese. With more money, we're richer. Isn't that better than sharing the money with foreigners?"

"It depends, Ed. The wealth of a society isn't measured by how many pieces of paper its citizens hold. If America does not trade with Japan, Americans have more pieces of paper. But do they have more goods and services and the leisure to enjoy them? Unless the Japanese send televisions to America out of the goodness of their hearts, then America has no Japanese televisions. Without Japanese televisions, America must make those televisions domestically. Making those televisions domestically requires people and raw materials. But the roundabout way of making televisions by making drugs and swapping them for televisions produces televisions more cheaply."

"The theory sounds pretty good, but how about some evidence? You claim that Merck can make televisions more cheaply using the roundabout way than I did with an old-fashioned television factory. Prove to me that televisions have gotten cheaper—and without using some fancy theory."

"Take it easy, Ed. Calm down. Back in 1960, how many hours did one of your workers have to work in order to earn enough money to buy a television set?"

"About two weeks."

"Today the average American can earn a TV in less than a day."

"You're kidding! But what about the quality? If you're going to compare a 1960s television to one made in 2005, you've got to compare televisions of the same quality. If those televisions are made in Japan, they couldn't be very good."

"I'll let you be the judge of that. Let's go back to Illinois and take a look."

"I suppose Willie's Appliance Store is gone."

"I'm afraid so. Replaced by a juice bar, a phenomenon we can explore later. But don't worry, you can still buy a television in Star."

Back in Star, I took Ed to a Circuit City to look at the televisions of the year 2005.

He was overwhelmed by the array of shapes and sizes. We went over to a 20-inch color model.

"Ha!" said Ed. "$100! That's not such a bargain. That's not much less than my TVs. You said the average worker could buy one of these in less than a day."

"The average worker can. Wages are a lot higher now than they were in 1960. That's why it's useful to think about how many days of work it takes a worker to earn a television—it gets rid of the effects of inflation on both wages and televisions."

"Less than a day. Amazing. And the sharpness of the picture is astounding."

"And unlike the older sets you are used to, Ed, these new models hardly ever break. And they all come with a remote control."

I also reminded Ed that unlike 1960, in 2005 color televisions were the rule rather than a rarity. Then I took him to look at the big screens. He stood in silence gazing at a 42-inch plasma TV.

"Where's the rest of it?" he asked quietly.

"That's the whole thing. I know. It's only 4 inches deep. They've figured out how to make them a lot thinner than they could in your day."

"And a lot bigger," Ed said, shaking his head. "How much does it cost?"

"It's $1400. The average American worker can earn one in about two weeks—just over 11 days. About what it took a worker in 1960 to earn a 20-inch TV. Not quite the same, is it?"

"I'm impressed, Dave. But as nice as these new televisions are, Dave, I can't believe America can't compete and make a product that's just as good. What happened to good old American know-how?"

"It's still functioning. It just got redirected to other more productive areas. It's like your typing skills—how could you give up typing when you were the best typist in the building? It was too costly for you to be your own typist. The gains to the factory from your superlative typing are less than the gains to the factory from your time spent managing it. It is the same with televisions. America could easily make the best televisions in the world."

"Then why don't we?"

"Because the resources it would take to make the best televisions are better spent making the best drugs and swapping them for televisions that other countries make."

"Maybe you're right, but how do you know? Who makes the decision not to specialize in televisions and to specialize in drugs instead? How do you know it's the right decision?"

"No one person makes that decision. That is what is hard to understand, but really rather beautiful. If some American could make the same quality television as the Japanese but at a lower cost, that person could become fabulously wealthy. Evidently, a better American-made television would cost more to make than the current Japanese televisions."

"How do you know?"

"If it could be done, someone would have the incentive to make such a television and become wealthy. To make such a television, you would have to pull engineers and manufacturing know-how out of other industries, such as aerospace, computers, and pharmaceuticals. The talent is better used in those industries."

"How do you know?"

"If it were not true, a television manufacturer could outbid those industries for the talent. Of course, a television manufacturer can always outbid those industries for the talent by paying a higher wage. But we do not see such a phenomenon occurring. Evidently, the wage necessary to draw skilled labor out of other industries and into televisions is so large, an American television cannot be sold at a price that is competitive with the Japanese price. It reminds me how people confuse international trade with the Olympics, Ed."

"The Olympics? How could trade be like the Olympics?"

"In the 1970s and the 1980s, the East Germans and the Cubans dominated the Summer Olympics, despite their small populations. Some Americans clamored for a better Olympic team. Of course America could win the gold medal in every Olympic event if it wanted to. America could mobilize a larger portion of her resources for training facilities and make sure that the best sprinters, high jumpers, and gymnasts pursued their craft full-time. A committee of experts could select the best potential athletes and pay them enough to get them to give up their best alternative job. Do you think that would work?"

"I don't see why not."

"I think it would work. America could win every gold medal that way. But would it be worth it?"

"Not necessarily. But what's that have to do with trade?"

"It's an example of the seen and the unseen and how what is seen doesn't capture the whole story. America would have some glory. That would be seen and apparent. What would go unseen are the activities and opportunities that were sacrificed to have the glory. It wouldn't be worth it. It wasn't worth it for East Germany or Cuba. Oh, the athletes involved lived pretty well. It was worth it for them. But while they were winning gold medals, the people of Havana and East Berlin were living in poverty and squalor. The free market would never have produced such outcomes. It took an authoritarian government to make a colossal blunder like that. A lesser, but similar, mistake would be to insist that America at least win the gold medal in the 100-meter dash because Americans have always won the 100-meter dash. Should America insist on making the best televisions in the world simply because it always has? If televisions can be made at a lower cost by the roundabout way, then America is better off producing them the roundabout way."

CHAPTER

Is Trade Good for America?

"While we're talking about the Olympics, Dave, if the Japanese are making large numbers of televisions, are they ahead of the United States?"

"Why would you care if America is ahead or behind?"

"But surely it is better to be ahead than behind?"

"Maybe. It depends on the nature of the contest and how you keep score. In the early 1990s, people often thought the Japanese were ahead if they looked at Japanese incomes converted from yen to dollars. But Japanese have to pay prices in yen. When they took into account the prices in Japan and what Japanese incomes could buy, the average American still had a higher standard of living than the average Japanese by about 34 percent in 2002."

"That's a lot closer than they were in 1960, I bet."

"You are right."

"Did they narrow the gap by dragging America down or by improving themselves?"

"Some American workers were harmed by Japanese competition between 1960 and today. But overall, America got wealthier—a lot wealthier. Both nations prospered. The biggest mistake people make when thinking about trade is that it's a fight over a fixed pie. But with trade, allowing the people of each nation to use their skills as productively as possible creates wealth—the whole pie gets bigger. Both parties are better off."

"Can you prove that America is better off, Dave?"

"I would start with the evidence of your senses. The array of goods in that Circuit City store was pretty impressive, wasn't it?"

"Yes, it was. There was nothing like that back in 1960. Somebody must be buying those appliances and televisions."

"You could also look at your children and your workers' children and see that their standard of living is much higher than your generation's. But you don't know whether they are typical or not. To know what has happened to America overall, you must look at wages or income for most or all of the population."

"What do you find?"

"The government collects wage data for what it calls 'production or nonsupervisory workers.' They make up about 80 percent of the workforce.

In 1960, the average worker in this group made $2.09 per hour. In 2004, the figure was $15.48 per hour."

"But what about inflation?"

"Good point, Ed. After taking into account higher prices, the seeming fivefold increase in wages was in fact 26 percent."

"Hmm. That's not a very impressive increase over almost 45 years."

"I agree. But there is a very misleading aspect of the comparison. In 2004, workers took much more of their income in the form of fringe benefits such as pension plans, health and dental insurance, and longer vacations. In fact, such forms of compensation more than doubled between 1960 and 2004. The right measure of a worker's well-being should measure all forms of compensation, not just hourly wages."

"What happens when you account for the increase in fringe benefits?"

"The government has a survey of wages and benefits that covers a wider array of workers than just production and nonsupervisory workers. It's virtually everyone other than federal employees. Real hourly compensation for this larger group increased by more than 90 percent from 1960 to 2004. So it almost doubled. But the broadest measure of economic well-being would be per capita gross domestic product—"

"That's a mouthful."

"It is. But it is the broadest measure of how productive and wealthy we have become. After inflation, that number increased over 166 percent between 1960 and 2004, much more than double what it was before. And all of those estimates underestimate how much progress was made because of how hard it is to measure inflation accurately when the quality of the items, like those televisions we saw, is constantly improving."

"So America did well. But how could that be, Dave? What about unemployment? When we closed down our plant and Zenith and Motorola closed down theirs, America must have lost a lot of jobs."

"No. America just lost certain types of jobs. Do you like corn, Ed?"

"Yes, I do."

"Do you grow your own corn?"

"No."

"But you could, couldn't you? But you don't, for the same reason you don't do your own typing. It looks like growing your own corn is incredibly cheap. You just have the cost of a little seed. But growing your own corn is in fact incredibly expensive because of the time it takes to weed, water, and fertilize. That time appears to be free, but it is costly. You have lost the opportunity to earn money at some other activity and using that money to buy corn. Or having the time for leisure. If you think of your household as a nation, you import corn. You produce it in the roundabout way just like America produces televisions."

"But what if I were really good at growing corn?"

"Even if you were a fabulous farmer, it could be cheaper for you to work at something else and buy corn instead of growing it. It depends on whether it takes fewer minutes to grow an ear directly, or to earn enough money to buy corn by working at some other job using the roundabout way. You could say that your household has 'lost' the corn-growing job. But this would be a silly way of looking at what has occurred. You have lost the job of growing corn and gained a more valuable opportunity."

"What does that have to do with the jobs in the American television industry? Aren't they gone?"

"The television jobs are gone. But they have been replaced by other jobs. Think about agriculture. In 1900, about 40 percent of the American workforce was in agriculture. By the end of the twentieth century, that number was under 3 percent. The proportion of the workforce needed to feed the American people fell dramatically, not because of imports but because of better technology. But did that technology cost America jobs? It cost America certain types of jobs, but the overall number of jobs increased tremendously."

"But didn't those farming jobs disappear, Dave?"

"Not in the way you'd think. A farmer didn't wake up one morning to find his overalls gone, his tractor vanished, and his fields of grain replaced by a shopping center. As technology improved, some farmers' incomes fell. Some farmers retired early. Others sold their farms to more efficient farmers. And some just struggled until retirement. But the biggest change caused by that technology was invisible. The dreams of the children of farmers changed. Those children saw that agriculture was not a booming industry. Even though their parents and grandparents had been farmers, they saw that farming was going to be less profitable than it had been. Some of them weren't thrilled about becoming farmers, anyway. They made plans to become salespeople, engineers, chemists, and pilots. And those jobs were available precisely because America made the decision to let the agricultural sector get smaller."

"You're saying that the people took different types of jobs."

"That's right. Some even went into a new industry called television. Can you imagine how poor America would be in 1960 or 2005 if America had made a decision back in 1900 to preserve the size of the farming industry in the name of saving jobs?"

"But the agriculture jobs we lost went to other Americans. It's not like we started importing food."

"What's the difference?"

"I don't know. It seems like the two cases ought to be different. When American farmers lose their jobs because other Americans figure out a new technology, at least the inventors who benefit are Americans. When American farmers lose their jobs because foreigners sell food to America more cheaply, the benefits go to foreigners."

"In fact, either way makes America better off."

"How?"

"In either case, America gets less expensive food with a smaller number of farmers. That is the important change. You see America losing jobs. I see Americans spending less on food—food is cheaper, and fewer Americans have to work in the food business. American consumers are better off. But so are most American workers. When consumers have less expensive food, they have more resources to spend on other things. Industries other than farming can now expand. And they can find workers because not as many Americans are needed to grow food. This allows Americans to make more of other things now that they don't have to make as much food. Let me ask you a question, Ed. Do you think it would be good for America if all disease disappeared and everyone were perfectly healthy until the age of 120?"

"Sure."

"Why do you answer so quickly? Aren't you worried about what would happen to the doctors? America would lose all those high-paying doctor and health care jobs."

"Oh come on, Dave. If we could get rid of disease, doctors shouldn't stand in the way. They would just have to find other things to do."

"And if America finds a cheaper way to make televisions by importing them?"

"It's just not the same. Cheaper televisions are not as important as getting rid of disease."

"But the principle is the same. Would a doctor have a right to force a person to stay sick so the doctor could continue earning the living the doctor was accustomed to? Does a television manufacturer have the right to force a consumer of televisions to pay a higher price to sustain high wages for his workers? But perhaps these are issues for a philosopher. In any case, we don't lose jobs if we eliminate disease or if foreigners sell America inexpensive televisions. Certain types of jobs are lost. If disease disappeared, we'd lose the medical jobs. People who would have been doctors would now apply their skills to other activities and enrich our lives and their own. Paradoxically, America would lose the high-paying jobs in health care but still become wealthier."

"And what about the people who are already doctors?"

"They would suffer hardship. The size of that hardship would depend on how disease disappeared. If it happened slowly, the hardship would be less, and medical workers would have time to adjust. If it happened literally overnight, it would be a lot crueler—to the doctors anyway. The sick would rather see disease disappear quickly."

"But when a factory closes, doesn't America have fewer jobs?"

"Just fewer jobs in that industry. The overall number of jobs in the United States exploded between 1960 and the end of the century. In 1960, there were 54 million jobs in the United States. By 2004, there were 131 million."

"Wow. That is amazing."

"Don't be misled. The ultimate reason jobs expanded was that the United States population was expanding, and a higher percentage of that population, particularly women, wanted to work. But the key point is that there were jobs for that expanded population, even though a lot of traditional American industries such as electronics, automobiles, and steel are smaller or have disappeared."

"What about my workers, Dave? What happened to the people who worked in my factory in Star?"

"The factory didn't shut down overnight. You struggled during the 1960s to compete with the Japanese. You finally sold your plants to the Japanese in 1975."

"I sold my factories to the Japanese?"

"They made you a good offer and promised to keep your factories open."

"Did they keep their promise?"

"Not exactly. They closed the plant in Star in 1978, throwing 4,000 of your workers out of work. You had laid off the other 1,000 before they bought you out."

"I can't believe I trusted them to keep their promise."

"They tried, Ed. The television market turned sour at the end of 1970s. There was price pressure on the Japanese. They kept your factory outside of Chicago open. They still run it, in fact."

"That's some consolation, I suppose."

"They don't do much of the work there, though. It's mainly an assembly plant. They import most of the components from low-wage Asian countries."

"What happened to those 4,000 workers when my factory closed for good? How does the roundabout way to wealth explain the poverty that must have followed? You can tell me that Merck is really a television company. And now that we've talked a little bit about the labor market, I understand what you were driving at. You were trying to tell me that the television jobs became higher-paying pharmaceutical jobs. But what about the transition? My assembly-line workers aren't chemists. When they lost their jobs, they'd need new skills and training. Some of them wouldn't be smart enough, or patient enough, to learn at their age. What happened to them?"

"Some retired. Some started their own businesses using the profit-sharing plan Stellar had in place. Some of those businesses thrived, and some failed. Some of your workers went to night school and acquired new skills. About a year after your plant closed, a couple of other factories opened in Star because companies knew of your workers' skills. Some of your workers found jobs there."

"And what about the wages my workers earned in their new jobs?"

"They weren't as high as yours. You were the best employer in town. Your workers loved you and your company, even after you sold out and the Japanese took over. They had a reunion of your workers ten years after the plant closed. Very bittersweet. They remembered the picnics, dinners, and good times. They had a lot of fond memories."

"But their new jobs paid less?"

"They did. Perhaps more importantly, as time passed, their wages didn't keep up with the wages in the rest of the American economy."

"But I thought you said that Americans got richer between 1960 and 2005."

"They did. But not every single person did better. And not everyone got richer at the same rate. Your workers' skills were relatively simple ones. Some of them had never finished high school. Only a handful of your workers—mainly the engineers—had been to college. A lot of workers suffered and struggled."

"I don't know, Dave. How can I face those people if I let that factory close? How do I explain to them that their jobs are going to disappear and the town we love is going to suffer in order for Americans to have cheaper televisions?"

"But you don't have to answer the question of why it's OK to destroy someone's way of life and someone's town for cheap televisions. It's a trick question. It's the wrong question."

"It may be the wrong question, Dave. But it's the one in my heart."

"I understand. Letting Japanese televisions into the United States will ultimately lead to lower prices for televisions. But that isn't the essence of free trade. The essence of trade is how it affects people's lives and the lives of their children. Think of a teenager working in your factory when it's doing well. She's working there part-time, thinking of dropping out of high school to work full-time. If she finishes high school, she might stay in town to work in your factory, or she might go on to college. When your factory closes down, she's more likely to go to college and certainly more likely to leave Star and—"

"But that's a horrible way of encouraging her! Shutting off her opportunities at home to justify shoving her out into the world."

"Relax, Ed. I quite agree. But that is not what I had in mind. She is more likely to leave Star for two reasons. The first is as you say. The closing of the factory is likely to push her out into the world beyond Star. But that isn't all. The world that she will inherit outside of Star—the choices and opportunities in the rest of the country—will not be the same if the factory disappears."

"Why is that?"

"If America trades freely with Japan and other nations, America gets more than cheap televisions and clothing and everything else that other countries can make more effectively than Americans. America gets a whole new set of opportunities for that girl and her generation to inherit. It is those opportunities that make leaving Star so attractive."

"How is she going to get to college if her parents don't have a job?"

"She'll have to go on scholarship or go to a state school or a community college, initially. But if she has ambition, she will find a way to fulfill it. By 2005, under free trade, the proportion of college-aged Americans going to college is higher than ever before."

"But what about the town, Dave? There are more jobs somewhere else in America. But there are fewer jobs here in Star. And I'll bet that a lot of other businesses besides mine struggled after my factory closed. And the jobs that are left don't pay as well. Star must be a shell of what it once was or what it could have been."

"Yes. But what happens to the town doesn't tell you what happens to the people who live here and the children they love. Star doesn't look as prosperous as it once was. But that is because the children of your workers will choose to find their opportunities elsewhere. The appearance of Star and all the manufacturing towns of America that are hurt by trade is a misleading one. To really see what has happened to those towns, you would have to take account of how the lives of the kids who left town have been transformed. You can't just look at what has happened to the towns alone. That would be as misleading as concluding that free trade reduces the number of jobs in America because a factory has closed. You've got to remember the roundabout way to wealth and remember that other businesses are expanding or getting started, creating opportunities tailored to the skills and dreams of the next generation."

"What happened to Jack Clements and his Ford dealership here in Star?"

"It closed. There wasn't enough money in the town to support it."

"That car dealership was his life, Dave. You can't know what it meant to him. Selling that dealership must have broken his heart."

"It did."

"How can that be good?"

"It was not good for Jack. But think about Jack's son, Danny. Remember him? He was Steven's childhood friend."

"I know that family well. Jack always dreamed of having Danny take over the dealership and settling down here in Star."

"Sure, that's what Jack wanted. But Danny had no dreams of running a car dealership. When Jack had to close it down, Danny was free."

"That's ridiculous. Closing the auto dealership didn't set Danny free. If he didn't want to work for his father, he didn't have to. He could always have done something else."

"Of course he could. But his options would not be the same. Just like the kids of the people who worked in your factory. Letting the American television industry die means other industries will thrive. Remember the example of agriculture. Do you think Jack Clements would have run an auto dealership for half his life if the government back in 1900 had committed to keeping 40 percent of the population in farming? It just couldn't happen. Danny's options expanded precisely because the opportunities in Star were less attractive."

"So where did Danny end up?"

"He ended up in Chicago working for an investment firm. He makes a very good living."

"Do you think that's any consolation to Jack Clements?"

"Probably not, but it might be if he knew the connection between his hardship and the opportunities available to his son. He sees his dreams dying. He sees the labor of 30 years, embodied in his auto dealership, turning to nothingness. He feels like a failure. But he is not a failure. He had a run of 30 good years and provided people with their cars and excellent service. He sees that dealership as his child, but he does not understand the relationship between the dealership and his real child, Danny. The death of that dealership, and the death of other economic ventures around the country, are what gives kids like Danny the opportunity to pursue their dreams. Can Jack at the age of 55 retrain himself to pursue a new career? Some older workers can, but, sadly, Jack cannot. However, new careers are available to his son precisely because Jack's opportunities, and the opportunities of others like Jack, have changed so dramatically."

"But Jack wanted Danny to settle down in Star."

"Danny won't now. Jack wanted Danny to run his dealership. He won't now. He wanted his dealership to be his legacy. It isn't. Danny is his true legacy. Is the life of Jack Clements a tragedy? I do not know. There is always an element of sadness when dreams are thwarted. But protecting Jack Clements and his dealership from failure thwarts the dreams of Danny Clements and the children of Americans who want the widest range of opportunity possible. To tell Jack Clements that his dealership cannot fail is to condemn Danny Clements to a static life of American-made products only, some first-rate, some indifferent, some poor. It is to close off boulevards of dreams for the Dannys of America because without change, success, and failure, the world becomes less rich."

"Money isn't everything, Dave."

"You are right. When I say 'rich,' I don't just mean monetary wealth. I mean all the ways that life can be rich—the satisfactions that come from a meaningful life. But monetary wealth does help people live longer, have more walks on the beach, retire early, and have lots of things that improve the quality as well as the quantity of life."

"So free trade causes suffering today, but the next generation does better?"

"No, no, no. Trade creates benefits today—lower prices for everyone and innovation and expanded opportunities for millions as capital and workers flow into the new products and services a nation can create by using trade as a way to leverage the skills of others around the world. Consumers and workers are better off. But not *every* worker is better off. Some workers are hurt by competition with foreign workers. But even those workers can find some consolation knowing that their children will inherit a better world."

"I don't know if I have your faith, Dave."

"Faith has nothing to do with it. Look at your life. You helped transform the world. You didn't cure cancer or invent the automobile. But you are and were part of a revolution of how human beings communicate and use information, a revolution that started with the printing press, went through the radio and then television, and kept going with the computer and the Internet."

"The computer? The Internet? What are they?"

"We'll have a chance to see them shortly. The point is that in the last half of the twentieth century, the world, with America leading the way, changed the way people communicate and entertain each other in ways that would be unfathomable to someone living 100 or even 50 years ago. That revolution closed a lot of factories along the way, just as trade did. When you opened factories in Illinois, other factories closed as you attracted workers and capital. When people dream of making a new product or making an old product better, they improve people's lives, and they change the economic landscape. If their dreams come true, they attract capital and workers away from other uses. You're worried about your workers and what you'd say to them. I don't blame you. But I doubt you'd like to speak to the CEOs, managers, and workers in all the new companies whose dreams will never come to pass because you chose to freeze the world as it is in 1960."

"Who decides which dreams come true?"

"No one person. No committee of experts. No government agency. New products must survive the market test—they must make consumers better off in some way, or no one will buy them. You can give those who dream of making the world a better place a chance to meet that test. Or you can side with those who would make sure America keeps every manufacturing job it ever had, who would have had America keep all the agricultural jobs, who would have frozen the economic landscape to make sure that Americans will always make televisions. To keep those jobs in place requires laws that stop dreams, laws that stop economic change. Without those laws, those jobs will disappear, but new dreams will open up with new and better jobs. Give better jobs a chance to come into being in America and in the rest of the world."

"Speaking of children, Dave, can I see mine? Steven always wanted to be president of Stellar Television. What's he doing?"

"Your son got involved with computers."

"Computers? Wait, I remember now, I *have* heard of them. A man tried to sell me one. I took the train up to Chicago and he showed me a warehouse as big as my factory back in Star. That's what he called it—a computer! It took up the whole warehouse. I asked him what it would do. He said it would do my payroll and keep track of my inventory. When he told me the price, I said, 'no thanks.' What a dead-end industry!"

"You are in for a surprise, then, and this time a pleasant one. Someone figured out how to shrink a computer to fit on your desk with plenty of room to spare. And it is unimaginably faster and cheaper than the one you saw."

"You're making this up."

"I'm not. Let's go see one. I think you'll like it."

"Was my son the man who shrunk that monstrosity?"

"No, but he put his own stamp on the industry. You'll see."

CHAPTER

Are Manufacturing Jobs Better Than Service Jobs?

I took Ed to see his son. He lived in Palo Alto, California.

"Strange house, Dave. Where are we?"

"California."

"You said a lot of the children of my workers did better than their parents. But I can't say this house is much bigger than my own. Is Steven doing better than his old man?"

"Steven bought this house for $800,000."

"Eight hundred thousand dollars! You're kidding! Or is it because of inflation?"

"Inflation is a part of it, but $800,000 is well above the average price of houses in America. It's an expensive house."

"And it's a nice house. But no house is worth $800,000."

"Evidently it was when Steven bought it. It's probably worth quite a bit more now. A lot of people want to live in California these days. It keeps the price of housing high. Let's see the den. I think you'll enjoy it."

We watched Justin, Ed's 13-year-old grandson, do his homework. Ed was rather confused at first. Justin sat on the couch in front of a big-screen television. A computer sat on a nearby desk. Justin would call out the name of a mathematical function, and a color three-dimensional representation would appear on the screen of the television.

"That is some screen, Dave. Who's working the controls?"

"Your grandson, Justin."

"How? Is there somebody behind the screen manipulating some knobs or dials?"

"No, Ed. The computer is able to recognize Justin's voice and respond to his commands. Your son Steven improved and perfected the technology that makes it happen."

Ed didn't say anything, just swallowed hard. Justin asked his dad if he could watch a video and his dad said OK, as long as Justin didn't watch more than a few minutes. Had to watch his eyes, his dad said.

"What's wrong with his eyes?" asked Ed.

"Don't worry. He's OK. There's a special medicine he takes. He's going to be fine."

"Where does Steven manufacture his computers?"

"Nearby. You'll find it ironic—he buys some of his parts from your old competitor, Motorola."

"Motorola?"

"When Motorola closed down their television assembly plants, they, too, turned to computers. But they make semiconductors—little pieces of machinery inside the computer that carry information at unimaginable speed."

"What happened to their workers?"

"Much like what happened to those at Stellar. Some retired early, others moved on, and some faced hardship with little or nothing to turn to. Some of them stayed on and learned how to design, make, and sell semiconductors. But you'll be surprised to know what happened overall. In 1960, Motorola had about 14,000 employees. Now, Motorola employs almost 70,000 people in the United States making semiconductors and wireless communications systems—phones you can carry in your pocket and use wherever you go. And they've become an international company, like so many others. Worldwide, they employ over 130,000 people."

"So I guess you're trying to tell me that America didn't lose those Motorola television jobs. We replaced them with something better in semi-whatevers."

"Well, America didn't really replace the jobs; rather, the people who would have taken those jobs did something more productive instead. But you've got the right idea. American creativity was unleashed to improve telecommunications and computers and a myriad of other fields that didn't exist in 1960. In fact, Star now has a number of firms that assemble components for computers that your son buys. And some of your workers work in those companies."

I had trouble dragging Ed out of there. Between beaming at his grandkid and watching *Toy Story*, which Justin turned on after finishing his homework, Ed was pretty comfortable in the den. I finally talked him into leaving. We still had to find Susan, and the night was passing.

"Why, I bet Susan has three or four kids by now. I wonder what her husband does?"

"I think you'll be more interested in what Susan does."

"Susan? She doesn't have to work for a living, does she?"

"I can't say whether she has to or not. But she chooses to."

"Is her husband a bum?"

"Not at all. The lives of women have changed quite a bit over the last 45 years. In 1960, there were 22 million working women. By 2004, there were 65 million. This wasn't just due to population growth. The percentage of women who worked went from 36 percent to 56 percent over the same time period."

"How could they all find jobs? A lot of my workers are women. But most jobs for women are telephone operators, teachers, and nurses. How did they all find work?"

"That's the great thing about the jobs market in America, Ed. As more and more women entered the workforce, they didn't all want to be working at the traditional female jobs. They wanted to try other things. And those other opportunities opened up for them. The jobs weren't in the traditional American manufacturing areas such as steel and automobiles. They were in the new areas that expanded in the service sector— health care, the financial sector, the pharmaceutical industry, and computers. People talked as if this process had started in the 1980s, but it was an old, old story that had been going on in America for at least 50 years—the steady growth of service jobs and the steady decrease in manufacturing jobs as a proportion of total employment. Manufacturing declined for two reasons. One was technology. New productions processes were invented that made workers more productive. The second cause was that those same processes allowed foreigners with little skill but low wages the chance to be as productive as some Americans were at assembling and producing manufactured goods. Both of those changes made the average American better off—those changes meant that manufacturing didn't need as many resources as had been needed before. That freed up people and capital to make new things."

"So how much did manufacturing employment change?"

"Between 1960 and 2004, the proportion of workers in manufacturing fell from 28 percent to 11 percent. And even the absolute number of workers in manufacturing fell, not just the proportion."

"Eleven percent! That's pretty frightening, Dave. America must not be making anything anymore."

"America still makes plenty of stuff. Even though there were fewer workers in manufacturing in 2005 compared to 1960, manufacturing *output* increased dramatically. It was about four times larger. It nearly quadrupled."

"How can that be?"

"The workers that remained were more productive. It wasn't that the less productive ones got fired. The workers that remained were given equipment that made them more productive. Not as many workers were needed as before to get the job done."

"But don't manufacturing jobs pay better than other types of jobs? Didn't it hurt America to lose all those high-paying jobs?"

"Service jobs sound menial and second-rate in comparison to manufacturing jobs. People think of flipping hamburgers or selling cosmetics. Some service jobs do pay less than the average. But many pay more. Lawyers, doctors, movie stars, computer programmers, financial analysts, consultants, and health care administrators are all part of the service sector. But manufacturing jobs do pay a little more than other jobs. In 1960, manufacturing workers made 12 percent more per hour than other private sector workers. By 2004, manufacturing wages were still 3.5 percent higher."

"So why would you want to lose the jobs that pay the most? You told me America has gotten wealthier between 1960 and 2005. But we would have been even wealthier if we had kept the proportion of jobs in manufacturing at 28 percent or even higher."

"The exact opposite is the case. If America had kept those manufacturing jobs, America would have gotten poorer."

"I don't believe it. Isn't it just arithmetic? If you lose the high-paying jobs you have to get poorer."

"It depends on why manufacturing jobs become less numerous. Who's the greatest basketball player in America?"

"That's easy. Wilt Chamberlain. What an athlete! I drove the family down to the University of Missouri a few years back so they could see him when he played for Kansas. No one could stop him that night. And no one stops him in the pros, except for maybe Bill Russell."

"Is Chamberlain a good shooter?"

"Not exactly, but he's a great *scorer*. He makes a very high percentage of his shots. It helps to be seven feet tall."

"So his shots go in more often than his teammates' shots?"

"Absolutely."

"Well then, his coach is a fool, don't you see? Why does he let the other players shoot? Wilt's team could score more points if he took all the shots!"

"Dave. You may be a good economist, but you don't know much about basketball. If Wilt the Stilt took all the shots, then eventually the other teams would catch on and would use all five players to defend against him. His shooting percentage would plummet. The threat and reality of his teammates' shots are what free Wilt up to be so effective."

"So you're saying that I can't assume that his shooting percentage is independent of how many shots he takes."

"That's right."

"It's the same idea with manufacturing, Ed. Not all manufacturing jobs pay well. Between 1960 and 2005, the manufacturing jobs that paid the least and required the least skill left America. It is precisely because the proportion of employment in manufacturing fell from 28 percent to 11 percent that the wage premium for manufacturing stayed as high as it did. The manufacturing jobs that were no longer in America weren't a random cross section of the manufacturing sector. They were the lowest-paying jobs requiring the least skill. If America had kept all the jobs in manufacturing, the manufacturing wage premium would have fallen for the same reason that Wilt Chamberlain would have a lower shooting percentage if he took too many shots."

"I guess you know more about basketball than I thought."

"I get around."

"But if new technology allowed low-skill workers to assemble products anywhere in the world, won't *all* the manufacturing jobs go to the countries with the lowest wages? Isn't it just a matter of time before even the high-paying manufacturing jobs go to foreigners?"

"Wages aren't all that matter. Otherwise all the jobs in America would end up in Mississippi or Arkansas."

"Excuse me?"

"The average wage rate in Mississippi is lower than the average wage rate in California. Or Illinois. Why didn't you move your television factory from Illinois to somewhere in Mississippi?"

"My workers in Star are highly skilled and reliable. I might not find workers as skilled and reliable in Mississippi. If I only cared about wages, I'd only hire teenagers. But not every teenager has the skills to work in a factory or manage the factory floor. It's absurd."

"That's right. Wages aren't all that matters. Productivity is just as important. The average American worker is much more skilled and productive than the average Mexican or Indonesian worker. Just because Japan, Mexico, or Thailand has lower wages than the United States does not necessarily mean that it's cheaper to run every factory there."

"But I can see why Americans would be worried about competition from low-wage nations."

"Sure. Americans were afraid of losing jobs to the Japanese back in 1960 when Japanese wages were a fraction of American wages. They worried about losing jobs to Mexicans in the beginning of the 1990s. And at the start of the twenty-first century, they worried about losing jobs to China and India where wages were much lower—decade after decade of worrying. Yet the worries that worried the worriers never came to pass. Despite decade after decade of worrying, America enjoyed decade after decade of steady growth in employment, decade after decade of an increased standard of living in America. The worriers always found buyers for what they were selling. Can you imagine what it must be like to be a poor peasant in China or Mexico or Indonesia and discover that the United States, the richest country in the world, is worried about competing with you?"

"That does seem a little strange."

"At the heart of those worries was a fundamental misconception about jobs and wages. People assumed that jobs were boxes that workers jumped into. If you're lucky, you find yourself in a box with a good wage. If you're unlucky, you get a bad box. In this view, the goal of a nation is to get the good boxes, the good jobs, the ones with high wages attached to them. And somehow, if we let foreigners sell things freely in the United States, they'll steal the good boxes, and America will be left with the bad ones. But wages and jobs don't work that way. If they did, then Haiti could become rich starting a pharmaceutical industry. Or America could increase its standard of living by creating enough new NBA franchises so everyone could become a basketball player."

"I don't understand, Dave."

"Basketball players make much more than the average, so if everyone were a basketball player, then, the average income in the United States would have to go up."

"That's ridiculous. The wages of basketball players wouldn't stay the same if there were thousands of teams."

"Exactly. It's the same flawed reasoning as those who argue that because manufacturing pays more than another sector, America can increase its standard of living by expanding manufacturing. A nation's standard of living depends on the productivity of its people, not the job titles they hold. The jobs people hold aren't random. They're the result of the skills and desires of the people in those jobs. Think back to the high-paying medical jobs that would disappear if disease were eliminated. Do you think the people who would have been doctors are now going to be street sweepers? They are not. They are going to take their skills and discipline to learn about something other than medicine. New industries are going to be created. And talented, hard-working people will get paid well. The wages aren't attached to the boxes or to the job titles. The wages go with the people."

"But when certain kind of jobs disappear, how do you know something new will come along?"

"Imagine a farmer in 1900 worrying about the decline in farming. Suppose he knew that in 100 years there would be only a trivial number of jobs in farming relative to what there were in 1900. Sure he'd be worried. He'd predict mass unemployment and starvation. He'd predict rioting in the streets. What could possibly replace a key American industry, the dominant American industry of the day—farming? But if he could see into the future and see the invention of the television, advanced farming techniques, and the myriad of other industries and products that America would enjoy and the new jobs that would arise in those industries, he wouldn't be worried at all. There is no limit to the human imagination. America's greatest resources are knowledge, know-how, and creativity. Such markets can never be cornered. There have always been occupations that use these skills, and there always will be. And those new skills and occupations are easier to create when you use the roundabout way to wealth and let people outside the United States produce some of the goods and services you once produced for yourself."

"I suppose service jobs aren't so bad. And at least they aren't at risk from foreign competition. You can't import a haircut. Or a physical from a doctor."

"That's what you'd think. And if that were true, the move away from manufacturing jobs toward service jobs would have made free trade less controversial by 2005. But it turned out a lot of services can be imported. It was all because of the Internet."

CHAPTER

Is Outsourcing a Threat to American Prosperity?

6

"The Internet? You mentioned that before. What is it, Dave?"

"It's a way of communicating information, ideas, and products over vast distances, all at once, to millions of people at the same time."

"I don't understand."

"Let's go see Susan. She works out of her house. Her business is related to the Internet."

"Some kind of crafts business?"

"Not exactly."

I took Dave to a suburb outside of Boston. We went over to a nearby park where Susan and her husband were watching their daughter play in a Little League game.

"Girls playing Little League, Dave?"

"I told you the world has changed a lot since 1960."

"Why does the ball sound so funny?"

"It's not the ball—it's the bat. It's made of metal."

"Metal bats?"

"Some are even made in Japan. They never break. It keeps the cost down."

"I don't know what's harder to get used to—girls playing baseball or metal bats." ✳

When the game was over, we watched Susan and her family walk back to their house. After watching the family eat dinner, Ed had a chance to see how the Internet worked. Susan had created a Web site that allowed clothes to be custom-fit using 3-D imaging. The site was linked to online clothing sellers and allowed customers to try on clothes online from the comfort of their home. I gave Ed a quick explanation of how the Internet worked, and with a little additional commentary from me, Ed was able to understand in some fashion what Susan was doing as she worked on her Web site.

"Susan did that?"

"With the help of some capital from investors and her cofounders, yes."

We watched Susan add some pictures to her family's home page from the Little League game. Then she paid some bills on line, e-mailed a

31

friend on vacation in Europe and looked up the words to an old song using Google. Ed was in awe.

"What's she doing now?" Ed asked.

"Downloading some songs to iTunes. Then she'll—"

"What's eye tunes?"

How do you explain iTunes and an iPod to a man in 1960 with a turntable and a stack of vinyl records? How do you explain how a man 40 years later could hold 10,000 songs in the palm of his hand? I did the best I could.

"This is a whole new world, Dave."

"Yes. The Internet is a great tool for research, shopping, business-to-business selling, keeping in touch with friends, finding new ones, and hearing new music. And its surface has only been scratched. Where it will go is impossible to forecast. But one thing is clear—American know-how is at the forefront of the Internet. Hundreds of thousands of good jobs have already been created. There will be many more to come down the road. But as marvelous as the Internet is, some Americans saw it as a threat to American prosperity."

"Why was that?"

"The Internet allowed people to communicate and work in new ways. One of the things it made possible was 'outsourcing.' Outsourcing once meant going outside your company for a particular service, such as hiring a specialized firm to handle your payroll or your legal issues. But eventually it came to refer mostly to hiring people outside of the country to do a job. So it wasn't just manufacturing jobs that were affected by trade but service jobs as well. Companies started hiring people from all over the world to provide their services."

"I don't understand. How could I hire a Chinese company to do my payroll?"

"That would be difficult. But things just as strange began to happen. News agencies hired Indian journalists to write headlines. Corporations hired foreign computer programmers to write their computer programs. Hospitals would even send X-rays to India to get them analyzed by Indian radiologists."

"But that would take forever! Who would want to wait for their X-rays to get to India, then have them analyzed by some Indian doctor and send them back to America?"

"That's where the Internet came in. The Internet let people send information around the world in an instant. You could send the X-ray to India and back in no time. Think of it as a telegram. But a telegram where you could send a picture or a video—"

"What's a video?"

"Sorry. A film. But it wasn't just words and pictures and movies that people could send around the world almost instantaneously. The most important thing that people worried about was the programs that made the computers work."

"Programs?"

"All those incredible things you saw Justin and Susan do with the computer used something called 'software'—the brains of the computer."

I explained to Ed some of the complexity of Web-page design, database administration, networking, and Internet security, the whole range of occupations created when the Internet became such an important part of people's lives.

"All that sounds wonderful, Dave. What was the problem?"

"It *was* wonderful. All these jobs paid well. But the Internet allowed programmers and software engineers and database people all over the world to compete with Americans. Suddenly a lot of companies were laying off high-paid American programmers and hiring less expensive programmers in India, instead. A company would ask an Indian company over the Internet to write a new software program. Just like manufacturing jobs, *knowledge* jobs were being done by people outside the United States for less money. One forecast said that millions of jobs done by Americans would soon be done by foreigners."

"I can see why that would scare people. It's one thing for foreigners to steal the lowest-paying manufacturing jobs that were best done overseas, but you're telling me that the highest-paying service jobs—computer jobs—were being stolen by foreigners. That's—"

"Whoa, Ed. Foreigners don't steal jobs from Americans. Some foreigners can do things more cheaply than Americans, and other Americans choose to hire them or buy the products they make. The jobs aren't 'stolen.' Remember that trade doesn't change the total number of jobs but rather the kind of jobs people do. But people called it 'stealing.' People said that if America didn't do something to stop outsourcing and all the good jobs supposedly going overseas, Americans would be left with the worst service jobs, they'd end up doing one another's laundry, selling each other makeup, and flipping hamburgers for each other. They also attacked me and my ideas."

"You! How?"

"They made fun of that theory we talked about earlier, the theory of comparative advantage, the one I wrote about in 1817 that you and I call the roundabout way to wealth. Said it was out of date. Old-fashioned. Nineteenth-century stuff. Said it didn't apply anymore. Said that I didn't anticipate a world where capital was mobile or a world of computers. Said that—"

"Well you couldn't anticipate those things, Dave. Those sound like cheap shots. Seems pretty unfair."

"It wasn't the unfairness that bothered me. It was the logic. The essence of comparative advantage—the roundabout way to wealth—doesn't depend on any of those things. I gave a simple example back in 1817 to describe the idea—two countries, England and Portugal, swapping wool for wine. But mobile capital or computers or more than two countries or two goods didn't change the fundamentals of that idea—that if someone can make something and sell it to you for less than it costs to make it yourself, you should trade for it rather than making it yourself."

"But that didn't change the fact that America was losing good-paying jobs that were now being done by foreigners, did it?"

"No, but that fact was deceiving. It only told half the story. Suppose one day a brand-new car appeared in the driveway of every American with the keys in the ignition and a card on the front seat guaranteeing free gasoline for life. And there's a note in the glove compartment saying that after five years, the car will be replaced by another free one. Would you drive that car? Would it matter whether it was a gift from an American or a foreign supplier?"

"Sure it would. If it were made by a foreign supplier it would mean the end of the American auto industry. You've told me that it has gotten smaller over the years. But free cars from foreigners would kill it."

"So if you were president of the United States you'd go on TV and the radio and warn the American people of the dangers of accepting the gift. You'd tell them it was a Trojan horse that would destroy the economy from within. You'd collect all those cars for a giant scrap drive in order to preserve the U.S. auto industry and American prosperity."

Ed hesitated. I could see there was something bothering him.

"What's wrong?" I asked.

"That does seem a little bizarre, destroying all those cars."

"Let's flip it around. Suppose you wake up in the morning, and there's no new car in the driveway—just the same one that you've been driving. But the president makes a similar speech. A government official will be coming to get your car and drive it off a cliff where the remains would be buried. Sure you're going to have to buy a new car, but employment in the U.S. auto industry will increase, and prosperity will follow, won't it? Or will it? Would that policy make America richer or poorer?"

"It would make Detroit richer."

"That's right. The auto industry would expand. But the country as a whole would be the poorer for it. You don't get rich destroying things. You get poorer. And the opposite is the road to prosperity. Free cars—or merely less expensive cars—make the country richer. Bad for Detroit. Good for everyone else. And the harm to Detroit would be offset not just by your happiness because you'd never have to pay for a new car again. The other effect would be what you'd do with the money you didn't have to spend on cars. And all the extra traveling you'd be doing with that free gasoline. A whole new set of activities would spring up. Some of those activities would use the workers from those abandoned auto factories.

But there'd be new opportunities for young people just entering the labor market as well."

"I see that."

"That's the part of the story that was missing when people complained about foreigners providing computer services at a lower cost than Americans. It did put some Americans in some industries out of work at first. But it let companies pay a lot less for computer services. Companies that couldn't afford computers before were now able to. Companies that already were using computers expanded their use of technology. The worriers ignored all those benefits and all the new things that became possible because Americans didn't have to spend as much as they did before to get computer technology. And as it turned out, only the lowest-paying computer jobs became less numerous. Those were the jobs that foreigners could do at a distance much more cheaply than Americans. Between 1999 and 2004, when the worries about outsourcing were at their peak, the number of computer programmers in America fell by 25 percent. But the number of software engineers rose by 50 percent, more than making up for the lost jobs in computer programming. Overall, the number of high-paying computer jobs rose by 17 percent, and the real wages of American workers in the computer industry increased as well. Outsourcing made most workers in the high-tech sector better off as demand for those skills increased."

"But what happens when foreigners figure out how to do *those* jobs at lower wages?"

"Why, there'd be nothing interesting left for Americans to do. Americans would just shrug, pick up their laundry detergent, and report to the massive laundromat where everyone would work."

"Now, Dave, don't—"

"Sorry, Ed. I don't mean to get frustrated. But your worry about what will come along to take the place of computer jobs is the oldest worry in the world. And it never, ever turns out to be true. Look at all the new jobs we've talked about tonight that didn't exist in 1960. In 2060, there will be a whole new bunch of jobs we can't imagine now that will come along and replace what Americans do today. The good jobs of today are going to disappear the same way that buggy manufacturers and leech ranchers disappeared. They will disappear because we will find new and cheaper ways to get things done. That's good."

"What's a leech rancher?"

"Sorry, I made it up. When doctors used leeches, there must have been people who raised them. I don't know what they were called. Something will come along in 2060 that will make today's medical devices look like leeches. And the creative people who come up with those new products will find the resources and time to find those new products because the world's wealth will grow and make those discoveries possible. There's one more thing people ignored when they worried about Indians learning how to do something once done by Americans."

"What's that?"

"Both sides benefit from trade. America gets wealthier using cheaper Indian computer programmers. But India benefits, too. Do we really want to use only American expertise when America can benefit from the skills of Indians? Do we really want to keep those poor Indians from using their skills in a bigger, richer market that demands their skills? Very cruel."

Ed was lost in thought for a while, trying to take in everything we had seen and discussed.

"I'm mighty proud of my kids, Dave. They seem to thrive in a world of international trade. It makes up for a lot after losing the factory and the changes that Star has gone through. The future looks pretty good from the present. But I've still got my doubts. Star is real ugly. All those parking lots, big stores, and hideous colors on all of the signs."

"The kids don't think so. To them it looks the way Star is supposed to look. If they were to live in the Star of 1960, they would find it archaic and quite ugly in its own way."

"Even so, though I'm proud of how my children have turned out, maybe life would have been better for them without all of these changes. For one, Susan might still be living in Star with more than one kid. And what about all my workers who lost their jobs? How do I know things might not have been better for them in a different world?"

Ed was loyal to his workers. I had an idea on how to give Ed more information, but it took an extension of my powers. I took Ed back to Star and over to where Willie's Appliance Store once stood and bought him a strawberry-banana smoothie. He rather liked it. While he worked on it, I excused myself and ducked Upstairs to make a special request.

CHAPTER

Do Tariffs Protect American Jobs?

7

"Hey, what happened? Where are we?" Ed asked.

Ed and I stood on the corner of Main and Oak in downtown Star, Illinois. The year was 2005, and we were standing in front of Willie's Appliance Store. Ed looked around.

"Now this is the Star I know and love," beamed Ed.

"Are you sure?"

"At least it looks and feels right. The buildings look the way they used to back in 1960, and the stores are all there. One thing is bothering me, though. Why are so many people driving Ford Fairlanes and Chevy Impalas?"

"That's all everyone drives."

"What happened to Chrysler?"

"They went out of business in the early 1980s."

"Why? And why do Ford and Chevrolet offer such a narrow range of products?"

"People couldn't afford to buy as many cars as they once did. You see, Ed, this is how Star will be in 2005 if America has no imports. This is what America will look like if Frank Bates becomes president and his second bill passes. His first bill 'protected' Americans from foreign televisions. His second bill eliminated all imports and will stay in force permanently. What you see around you is a self-sufficient America. But without imports, America has to devote a lot of resources to make things they hadn't made before. Those items got so expensive, people could not afford the same cars as they did before. It all started with televisions. You got your bill passed—"

"It wasn't my bill, it was Frank Bates's bill."

"But you gave him the idea. When that bill passed, your company did exceedingly well: Sales went up, production went up. You hired more workers. To get them to leave their previous jobs and come work for you, you increased the wages you paid. Star was booming, and everybody could see it. There were new buildings going up all over town. Your workers were driving Cadillacs and Lincoln Continentals. Some were driving Corvettes. They dressed well. They built themselves fancier and fancier houses."

37

"So what was wrong with that? It sounds pretty good."

"It was. For your workers. But overall, Americans were harmed."

"I disagree. Completely. First, if someone gets richer, how does it hurt others? You told me earlier that when Japan got rich, it didn't hurt the United States."

"Getting rich doesn't have to impoverish someone else. But it can, as we shall see. Second?"

"Second, we've talked a lot about how we don't lose jobs when we import goods. If I understand the argument, we only lose those types of jobs. But you admitted that imports cause dislocation and hardship for some."

"In the short run, yes. And I also admitted the short run may not be so short for some people."

"Then it seems to me that a pretty good case can be made for restricting imports in some fashion. It prevents that short-run hardship."

"Some hardship is inevitable when we let people buy what they want, trade with whom they want to, work for whom they want to. It has nothing to do specifically with international trade. When people decide to reduce the amount of carbohydrates they consume, bakers have to react. Some come up with low-carb bread, but others will have to do something else. When the population gets older, some products become more popular, and others inevitably fade away. A free society is dynamic—it's alive. A thriving and dynamic economy means some people inevitably have to adjust to the changes that come with life. The hardship that comes with the freedom to make choices is linked inextricably to the benefits. Without that hardship you don't unleash any of the benefits of the roundabout way to wealth— the opportunity for people to use their skills in the most productive way possible, the lower prices that people pay, creating new opportunities with the resources left over. No short-run benefits. No long-run benefits, as each generation gets to use its skills to the utmost. But more importantly, I am going to show you that you cannot avoid hardship by restricting imports. Let us start by examining the workings of a tariff on televisions."

"But Congressman Bates's bill wasn't a tariff. It just limited foreign imports. And it was for my workers' protection."

"I know, Ed. You asked for a quota. But it turns out that a tariff and a quota are virtually the same."

"How can that be? The tariff is a tax that applies only to foreign-made goods. But a quota doesn't force the foreign manufacturers to raise their prices the way a tariff does. It merely limits what they can sell at the old price. It's much more fair."

"We shall see, Ed. Let us begin with a tariff. A tariff on imported televisions increases the price of both foreign and domestically produced televisions. It expands the market of American television producers and contracts the market for foreign-made televisions."

"Wait a minute, Dave. Why does it raise the price of domestic televisions? The tariff isn't on domestic televisions, just foreign ones."

"Funny, that's what every American automobile executive says when asking for a tariff on foreign cars. 'We would never change our prices just because of a tariff.' Strangely enough, this promise is always broken."

"Why? How can they raise prices when they don't have to pay the tax?"

"Let's stick with televisions. Suppose that before the tariff is imposed, domestic and foreign televisions with the same features and roughly equal quality are selling for $250. Now the American government imposes a tariff on foreign televisions of $25. A tariff is just a fancy word for a tax on goods made by foreigners. A $25 tariff means that every foreign company that sells a television in the United States must pay $25 to the U.S. government."

"So the manufacturer increases the price to $275 so the manufacturer can make $250 just like before."

"Not so fast. The manufacturer would like to increase the price to $275. A price of $300 would be even better. But what a manufacturer would like to do and what a manufacturer is able to do are not necessarily the same. Competition among suppliers constrains the power of the profit urge."

"But foreign televisions do get more expensive, don't they?"

"Yes, they do. Otherwise it won't be worthwhile for foreigners to bring televisions to America, given that they have to pay a tariff in America. Let's not worry about the exact amount for now. When foreign-made televisions get more expensive, people who used to buy the foreign-made televisions will want instead to buy the American televisions of the same quality that are now cheaper in comparison. When more people want to buy something than before, the price goes up."

"But that's not fair, Dave! The American manufacturer hasn't been hit by a tax. It has no right to raise the price. Its costs haven't changed."

"Perhaps it seems unfair. But consider the alternative. Suppose the American manufacturer does not increase the price. What will happen?"

"It will make the same amount per television as it made before. Seems fair."

"But if it makes the same amount per television as before, will the manufacturer expand the output or keep it unchanged?"

"Keep it unchanged. You're not going to open a new factory and expand your capacity without a higher price. You would have already opened all the factories that would be profitable at the old price."

"Exactly. But while domestic television production is unchanged, Americans want to buy more domestic televisions than they did before because of the price increase of foreign-made televisions. Too many consumers are chasing too few televisions. What do you think is happening in the stores?"

"Customers are finding that the television they planned to buy is gone when they get to the store. Consumers will be lining up before the stores open to be sure to get the television they want to buy."

"So the true price of buying a television has already gone up. If the seller of American televisions does not raise the price on the televisions, the true price increases anyway because the buyer must now sacrifice time waiting in line to buy a television."

"I guess the seller would raise the price after all. Even at the higher price, the seller can sell the same number of televisions as before because the competition from abroad was hit with the tariff."

"Very good, Ed. In fact, even if the seller failed to notice the lines outside the shop, customers would drive prices higher by offering a higher price in order to avoid standing in line."

"OK, OK, so the price of both American and foreign televisions rises with a tariff."

"In fact, as you guessed, both prices will often rise by the full amount of the tariff, for reasons we need not explore. In our example, the $250 television has become a television selling for $275, whether it is made in America or abroad. American producers expand output in response to the increased demand for their product and the higher price. New American television factories are opened. The demand for workers with the skills to work in a television factory goes up. So do their wages."

"Sounds good for America. Higher wages and more jobs."

"It is good for some Americans. Your workers, for example, and your stockholders. The increase in the price of televisions makes them better off. Is anyone worse off?"

"I guess people who buy televisions have to pay more than they did before."

"Exactly. Some Americans continue to buy foreign televisions at the new price of $275. Others buy American-made televisions at the same price. The increase in price makes consumers of televisions worse off. What happens to the extra $25 they are now paying for televisions? The extra $25 paid to foreign suppliers gets recaptured by the American government in the form of tariff revenue. The extra $25 paid to American manufacturers increases their profits and the wages of their workers."

"Is that wrong, Dave? If the benefits in the form of tax revenue and higher profits and wages cancel the losses, it seems like a wash."

"On the surface it appears to be a wash. Of course, it means that those Cadillacs and Lincolns your workers were buying with their higher wages were paid for out of the pocket of the American television consumer. Each consumer had to give up $25 worth of some good so that your workers could prosper. The gains to workers look larger because there are fewer of them compared to the number of buyers of televisions.

So while the loss by each consumer of televisions is only $25, the gain to each worker is much, much larger."

"I still don't see what's wrong with that."

"One could argue that it is a form of extortion. Your workers took money from the pockets of television buyers. How? Not by making a better product or because there were not enough televisions to go around due to increases in your cost but merely because the government restrained your competition. But that is a philosophical issue we perhaps should set aside. Surely you can see how the fancier cars your workers drove gave a false impression of a higher quality of life for Americans. You just don't see the poorer standard of living for the television buyers. Some Americans benefited, but others lost."

"OK, OK. Some Americans are better off and some are worse off. Maybe the gains to those who win are bigger than the losses to those who lose."

"Alas, in fact, the losses outweigh the gains."

"How do you know, Dave?"

"Every television, imported or domestic, is $25 more expensive than it used to be. So every buyer of televisions has lost $25 relative to a world without the tariff."

"But, Dave, hasn't every producer gained that $25? It still seems like a wash."

"Not quite. The gain to the American producer is less than $25."

"Come on, Dave. How can a $25 loss not be somebody's $25 gain?"

"Paradoxical, isn't it? Here is why, Ed. If you did nothing in response to the higher price of televisions, then your profits on each television would indeed be $25 higher, and the losses of the consumer would be offset by your gain. But the increase in the price of televisions encourages you to make more televisions. You expand production at your existing plant and perhaps build an additional one. But the costs of those additional televisions are not going to be the same as the costs of the smaller number you made before. The new televisions you make will be more costly. Your profits on the new televisions you make will be less than $25."

"Why?"

"Because you will not be able to run two factories as efficiently as one, for example. The manager you hire for the second plant will not be as skilled as the first, and you will not be able to keep an eye on two plants as well as you did when there was only one. As a result, your profits on those new televisions will be less than $25."

"But sometimes expanded production leads to lower costs. Haven't you heard of economies of scale, Dave?"

"I have kept up over the years, Ed. Yes, I have heard of economies of scale. But why would you wait for a tariff to expand your production and lower your costs? The wise manager will have already exhausted any available economies of scale. Additional expansion in response to a tariff will raise your costs. And that is why a tariff is not a wash for America as a whole. The harm to consumers is larger than the benefit to producers and their workers."

"How can that be, Dave? I still don't quite see how the losses and gains don't balance out."

"You have to remember how people respond to incentives. Your company responds to incentives by expanding production. That means more resources get devoted to televisions. That is not free. You use up more American resources in your bid for television sales that have gotten $25 more lucrative than they were before. America as a whole is poorer."

"Is that the end of the story?"

"No. Television manufacturers are not the only ones responding to incentives. Let us look at the chain of events again. The tax on foreign-made televisions increases the demand for American televisions and reduces the demand for foreign televisions. The price of American-made televisions also rises. American production expands, but imports have fallen. What happens to the total number of televisions bought by Americans? It falls, even though American production has gone up. The reduction in imports always outweighs the increase in production from American sources."

"Why?"

"Because the overall price of all televisions, domestic or foreign, has gone up. Nothing has happened to change the number of televisions people want to buy except an increase in price. When televisions are more expensive, people want to buy fewer of them. Americans, taken as a whole, are worse off because they have fewer televisions to enjoy."

"Wait a minute, Dave. If Americans had fewer televisions, then they had more of something else. You're saying that while some Americans were harmed by the increase in price and lost $25, some stopped buying televisions entirely. But this means they had the $250 they used to spend on televisions left over to buy something else with. So they had more of something else."

"Quite right. But we know that whatever they buy with the $250 is not as valuable to them as the television was."

"How can you tell?"

"Let us say a man who used to buy a $250 television now buys a suit of clothing instead. Before the tariff, he had the freedom to spend $250 on either the suit or the television and chose the television. That choice tells us that he gets more pleasure or usefulness from a television than he does from the suit of clothes when they both have the same price. By placing a tariff on televisions, you eliminate this choice. Instead, you force him to choose between a suit of clothes at $250 and a television for $275. You have forced him to swap the television for a suit of clothes, an exchange that makes him worse off. His loss is the difference in enjoyment between the two."

"At least you admit, Dave, that the tariff produced more American jobs."

"I beg your pardon?"

"I said at least you'll admit that the tariff created American jobs."

"Ed. You're a fine man, an intelligent man. But after all we have been through together, how can you say that a tariff produces jobs?"

"Doesn't it? I hired more workers than I did before, didn't I? Isn't that an increase in jobs?"

"Ed, do you remember the roundabout way to wealth?"

"Sure."

"What is it?"

"Sometimes it's cheaper to produce televisions in the roundabout way than the direct way. There are two ways to prod—"

"All right. Do you see a relationship between what we are talking about now and the roundabout way to wealth?"

"Not really. The roundabout way is a theory about production costs. My increase in workers and their wages isn't some abstract theory. Those changes are real. Those are real cars they're driving. The increase in jobs has to be good for America."

"Really? Let's go back to Rahway, New Jersey."

So we closed our eyes and headed to the northeast again.

"What do you see, Ed?"

"Nothing."

"Do you know where we are?"

"Looks like a corn field."

"It is. This corn field stands where the Merck pharmaceutical company used to stand."

"Where did it go?"

"Nowhere. It was never built in the first place. Remember, we are in the year 2005 when there are no imports because all foreign products are banned. Without free trade, this particular Merck plant never got built. Overall, there are fewer pharmaceutical companies and fewer jobs in the pharmaceutical industry."

"Why, Dave? And what's that have to do with a tariff on televisions?"

"When America makes goods for herself instead of importing them, some American factories expand, giving the impression that jobs are being created. All the things that America once imported will have to be made by Americans now—televisions and shoes and watches and everything else. But the people to fill those jobs have to come from somewhere."

"Come on, Dave. Are you telling me that because America stopped importing televisions and expanded domestic production, Merck never built this plant?"

"Yes."

"How can that be?"

"In a sense, there is absolutely no relationship between a television factory expansion and a pharmaceutical plant that is never built. Yet they are intimately related in so many ways. Because you and other American television manufacturers hired workers for your plant, this plant didn't have the workers available to staff it."

"But, Dave, you admitted before that workers in a television plant can't become chemists overnight. So how can chemists turn into television manufacturing workers overnight?"

"Overnight, no. But their children can, don't you see? And not everyone who works in a pharmaceutical company is a chemist. With free trade, some of your workers found work in the companies that expanded because of trade opportunities—either exporting companies that expanded or firms that sold to Americans who now had resources available to spend elsewhere. And some of the children of your workers became chemists and marketing people working for Merck and the other companies that expanded. Without free trade, making televisions suddenly looks more attractive than studying chemistry. The children of your workers didn't go on to graduate school to study chemistry."

"Why not?"

"Because the wages of chemists were less than they would be under free trade. There will still be chemists, just not as many as there would be under free trade."

"Why?"

"Two reasons. First, as you admitted earlier, when there is an expansion of the television industry, the wages of television workers rise. But the second reason is less obvious. Without imports, the demand for pharmaceuticals, via the roundabout way, is less than it was with free trade. As a result, the wages of chemists are lower than they were with free trade."

"Why is the demand lower?"

"When America allows free trade, America has fewer jobs in the television industry and more in the pharmaceutical industry. America doesn't get to keep all of the drugs its pharmaceutical industry produces—some of those go to Japan in exchange for televisions, remember?"

"Sure. So when there's free trade, some of those pharmaceutical workers are essentially making televisions, right? The roundabout way to wealth."

"Excellent, Ed. So what happens when America stops importing televisions?"

"The demand for American televisions goes up, and employment increases. I see that. I still don't see why the pharmaceutical jobs have to decrease."

"You're so close. Two reasons. The television workers have to come from somewhere. And those workers will be freed up from the pharmaceutical industry because demand from Japan for drugs will fall."

"That's what I'm having trouble seeing. Don't the Japanese still want life-saving drugs?"

"Of course. But what will they use to buy those drugs?"

"Dollars."

"And where will those dollars come from? Remember, Americans won't be buying any Japanese televisions. Before trade restrictions, America produced some of its televisions in the oundabout way. America produced drugs and swapped them for televisions. If fewer Japanese televisions come into the United States, the Japanese have fewer dollars. They, or the nations that trade with Japan to get dollars, will buy less of those things that dollars can buy, such as pharmaceuticals. American exporting industries will suffer."

"I don't know, Dave. It's hard to believe that just because there are fewer American dollars in the hands of Japanese people, they are going to be less interested in buying American pharmaceuticals."

"The money hides the real interaction between Americans and Japanese. Suppose you are a farmer. You grow food. By specializing in food, you get very good at growing it. There's a tailor in town who is good at making clothes. You barter with the tailor, swapping some of the food you grow for the clothes the tailor makes. One night, before going to bed, you take a stupidity potion. You wake up stupid and say, 'I'm not going to let those clothes-making jobs get out of my household. I am going to ban imports of clothing.' So you announce to the tailor in town that you are no longer going to buy any more of his clothing. What do you think happens to your sales of food to the tailor?"

"They're going to go down."

"They're not just going to go down. They're going to disappear. Can you see why?"

"If I don't want his clothes, he has nothing to offer me for my food."

"Exactly. Your refusal to import clothes is equivalent to saying you don't want to swap clothes for food. And you're not going to make up for the lost food sales to the tailor by selling food to, say, the carpenter who works on your house. The carpenter isn't any more interested in your food than he was before. The same thing is going on when the United States puts a tariff on televisions. America is saying to the world, 'We don't want to trade as much as we did before.' As a result, the United States is going to make more televisions and less of something else. America makes less of whatever it is Americans used to swap with foreigners for those televisions. Imports and exports are inextricably tied together."

"So the increase in American television workers is offset by a decrease in workers in industries that shipped goods to Japan or to some other foreign nation."

"Exactly. And that is why a tariff does not avoid the short-term hardship caused by foreign competition. A tariff creates its own short-run hardship. It is just harder to observe."

"Is the offset exact? Are the number of television jobs gained exactly the same as the number of export jobs lost?"

"That is really the wrong question. The number of jobs in America is determined by the population and the proportion of the population wanting to work. The real issue isn't the number of jobs but the kind of jobs people are doing. America should have its citizens work in the areas that allow the best application of their skills. Otherwise, there are lost opportunities to create wealth. A tariff creates two kinds of losses for Americans. Because televisions have become more expensive, too few televisions are purchased by Americans. The televisions that are still enjoyed by Americans are produced at an inefficiently high cost. America devotes more resources to producing televisions domestically than are necessary."

"Why, Dave?"

"The Merck pharmaceutical factory that once produced televisions in the roundabout way has been replaced by a Stellar television factory making televisions the direct way. Do you remember how Merck produces a television? They produce drugs sold in Japan. Take one of Merck's pharmaceutical products, one particular drug. There is some number of doses of that drug, that when sold in Japan, earns enough yen to purchase a television. Selling that number of doses in Japan is equivalent to producing a television by the roundabout way. The cost of producing that number of doses is lower than your cost of producing a television the direct way. Merck produces a television more efficiently. You could take the resources from your factory, turn them into a pharmaceutical factory, and still have resources left over for America to produce something else of value."

"I saw before that televisions did get a lot cheaper under free trade. Let's go look and see what happens to the price of a television when they are produced the direct way."

I took Ed back to Willie's Appliance Store, where we looked at some year 2005 televisions when no televisions were allowed to be imported. They were smaller, there were fewer choices, and they were a lot more expensive than they were at Circuit City under free trade.

"But why, Dave, why? Why are they so expensive?"

"It is that old theory of comparative advantage we talked about before—the roundabout way to wealth. Is the farmer who makes his own shirts richer or poorer? He looks richer because he has kept the shirt industry within his household; but in fact, he is poorer. Because he fails to concentrate on making food, he becomes a poorer farmer. Making the shirt is expensive because it means giving up time and skills better spent at farming. That is the America you see around you today with trade restrictions. It is a country that must do everything for itself. There are not enough people, machines, and land to go around to make everything as cheaply as could be made under free trade. All the skills that were unleashed in pharmaceuticals, computers, and—"

"What about my son Steve?"

"We will go see Steve. But before we do, I want you to think about the factory in Rahway that never was."

"The pharmaceutical plant?"

"Yes. In many ways it is the essence of the matter."

"Strange that something that doesn't exist should be the essence of the matter."

"When imports cause a television factory to lay off workers, we understand their pain and suffering, and feel sympathy for them. But when a tariff eliminates jobs at a pharmaceutical plant, the relationship is such a roundabout one that no one even notices it when it occurs. No one blames the tariff for the hardship in Rahway, but hardship is there nevertheless. Everyone believes that a tariff prevents the unemployment of the television or automobile workers. They don't see the tariff causing the unemployment of the pharmaceutical workers. The tariff is praised when the television plant is built. No one sees the pharmaceutical plant or computer plant that is never built. It is hard to see something that doesn't exist.

"And here is another irony, Ed. An American who buys an American car congratulates him- or herself for helping to provide American jobs. Never mind that the car is actually built in Canada or Mexico, or that half or more of the parts in the car are imported. American auto manufacturers have convinced most people that buying American is good for domestic jobs. But do you see the irony? An American who buys a Japanese car is also helping to create American jobs, but not in the car industry. The buyer of the Japanese car stimulates those industries that trade with Japan. The buyer of the Japanese car helps the Boeing worker, the chemist at Procter & Gamble, the Merck worker, the Disney cartoonists, and the workers in those industries that export American know-how around the world. It is not a question of creating jobs, but which jobs to create."

"I see the irony, Dave, but you can see how hard it is for people to see the full effects."

"I do. And that explains much of the politics behind trade protection. When Frank Bates pushes a bill to help the television industry, who favors it?"

"My workers, for one."

"How intense is their support?"

"A lot is at stake for them. They will write Frank letters and go see him when he visits from Washington. Their union will make contributions to Frank, and the workers will vote for him next election."

"Who should oppose Frank's bill, Ed?"

"Consumers."

"That's right. But the interest of the consumer is quite weak. The consumer has only $25 or so at stake, not the hundreds or thousands of dollars that your workers are fighting for. Naturally, the consumer is less motivated to get involved. Consumers feel guilty getting involved. All they hear over and over again is their patriotic duty to support domestic industry. Tell me, Ed, what do you think is a consumer's patriotic duty?"

"I thought I knew. But I see now that it is more complicated than I once thought. I would hope people would buy my televisions. But if they don't, I guess it doesn't hurt America, it just hurts some Americans and helps others."

"But many consumers don't see that, so they feel guilty buying foreign products or fighting trade protection. Of course, there is another group besides consumers who should fight protection."

"Those Merck workers, right?"

"Correct, Ed. Unfortunately, their opposition is muted."

"Why?"

"For one, while it is obvious that television workers stand to gain from a tariff on imported televisions, it is not always obvious which industries are harmed. Even worse, they may not even exist to fight for their self-interest. A law that preserves the television industry but harms the computer industry should be opposed by the workers in the computer industry, for example, who will not have the opportunities they would have had. But they may not be working in the industry yet. Take Steven, your son—"

"Can we go see him, Dave?"

"We will see him, Ed, I promise. Soon. But think of the Steven of 40 years ago, the Steven of 1960. In 1960, Steven is a child. He doesn't see how the protection of the television industry hurts the companies that trade with the rest of the world. He can't see how protection brings resources into the television industry and prevents other domestic industries such as computers from expanding. How can you expect him, child or adult, to oppose a law whose effects will not be felt for 30 years? But someone should be looking out for the children to make sure they have the opportunity to pursue their wildest dreams. Don't you think so, Ed?"

CHAPTER

8

Tariffs versus Quotas

"That's all well and good, Dave. But Frank Bates's original bill was a quota, not a tariff. They seem pretty different to me."

"There is a difference, but I doubt we're thinking along the same lines. What do you think the difference is?"

"A tariff is like a tax on foreigners. But a quota just reduces the amount of foreign supply that can come in. A quota gets the American consumer to substitute an American-made product for the foreign one."

"Ed, what do you think happens when there are fewer foreign televisions available?"

"Foreign televisions get more expensive, I'd guess."

"And with fewer foreign televisions available at a higher price, what do you think happens to the demand for American televisions?"

"It goes up. And so will the price, won't it, Dave? Hmm. It does sound something like a tariff."

"In fact, the same chain of events occurs with a quota that happens when a tariff is imposed. In response to the higher price for their product, domestic television producers expand their production. Both American and foreign-made televisions end up being more expensive. With an increase in price, consumers are harmed. Americans have fewer televisions to enjoy than they did before, and too many televisions are made domestically using the direct way while too few are made the roundabout way."

"I'm still confused about why the total number of televisions has to go down. Why can't the expansion of American production make up for the lost foreign imports caused by the quota?"

"Here's why. With a quota, there is a reduction in foreign supply, causing an increase in the price of televisions. In response to the increase in price, American production expands. But it can never equal or outweigh the reduction in foreign supply. Suppose it matched the decrease in foreign supply. Then the total combined supply of domestic and foreign televisions to U.S. consumers would be back to where it was before. If production is back to what it was before, then the price will be the same as it was before the quota; but then you would have a contradiction. Why would American manufacturers like yourself have expanded production if the price ends up unchanged? And if you do so by mistake, you will close some plants when you see that the new price is equal to the old one.

Not all of those new plants can be profitable at the old price, or you would have opened them before. The net effect of a quota is a decrease in supply and a higher price of televisions, both domestic and imported."

"It does sound a lot like a tariff."

"In fact, you can structure a quota to mimic a tariff perfectly. Suppose America imports 20 million televisions in the absence of tariffs and quotas. Suppose that when you put a tariff of $25 in place, the price goes from $250 to $275 and imports fall by 25 percent to 15 million televisions. You can have the exact same effect on the price of televisions by limiting the number of foreign televisions to 15 million. Price will go up to $275, just as it did under the tariff."

"Is there any difference between a tariff and a quota in those two situations, Dave?"

"A quota of 15 million mimics almost all of the effects of a $25 tariff in the example I described. In both cases, televisions in the stores will sell for $275. The difference is that in the case of a tariff, part of that higher price is captured by the American government in the form of tariff revenue."

"How does that work?"

"With a $25 tariff, the importer of the televisions has to pay the government $25. So while the consumer loses $25 on the imported televisions, at least some American will be the beneficiary of the $25 worth of government revenue when it is spent. Remember that from the standpoint of looking at all Americans, the gains and losses from the $25 by itself cancel out."

"Why do you say 'by itself'?"

"Because the money changing hands from the consumer to the government to the beneficiary of government spending *is* a wash. One American, the consumer, is $25 poorer, while another American, the beneficiary of government spending, is $25 richer. Whether that transfer from one American to another is fair is a separate question."

"But if one American gains and another loses, don't those differences cancel themselves out for America as a whole?"

"The money changing hands cancels out. But what is not a wash is the effect of that $25 transfer on people's behavior. Fewer televisions get enjoyed, and America devotes too many resources to producing televisions directly instead of through the roundabout way. That is not a wash. That is a net loss that makes America poorer. Suppose people without cars in America start stealing cars. In one sense, theft simply puts the cars in the hands of the thieves instead of in the hands of the people who bought them originally. You might think that theft is just a wash, a transfer, a mere rearrangement of resources. But that ignores how people respond to the possibility of threat. You lock up your car in the garage, you lock the doors of your car, you put antitheft devices in your car, you ask your local politician to put more police on the street.

All of those responses cost real resources, time and money and people that might be more productive elsewhere in the economy. A tariff or a quota does the same thing. They do more than cause money to change hands. They change domestic production and consumption. They make America poorer."

"So how does the quota differ from a tariff?"

"In the case of the quota, you still get the losses from too few televisions purchased and too many resources going to produce televisions directly. But the extra $25 paid by the consumer for the foreign-made televisions goes either to the American importer who brings in the televisions from abroad or to the foreign producer. If it is the latter, the foreign producer has 25 more American dollars to buy up pharmaceuticals, computers, and other American products."

"What's wrong with that?"

"With a tariff, that $25 of purchasing power and claims on American goods and services stays in American hands. With a quota, that $25 may end up in the hands of foreign producers. This allows foreigners to lay claim to American goods and services, leaving fewer computers, drugs, and other goods for Americans to enjoy. A tariff makes sure that those goods stay in American hands."

"But you told me before that when foreigners have dollars, they stimulate the American companies that export, such as Merck and Boeing."

"They do, but it would be better for America if foreigners kept the dollars and never 'stimulated' our economy. America would much rather have free televisions than have to swap drugs and airplanes for them. Then Americans would be able to enjoy more drugs and airplanes instead of the Japanese. But Japan isn't interested in giving away televisions. They expect something in return. In the case we are discussing, the question is: Who will have $25 to spend, Americans or foreigners? It is always better for America if Americans have the extra $25 instead of foreigners. That way the extra $25 worth of goods stays in America instead of going to Japan."

"What determines whether Americans running import businesses or foreign suppliers get to keep the extra $25?"

"It depends on how the quota is structured. Under a standard quota, the government hands out licenses to importers giving them the right to import a particular amount of the good being restricted. Under this system, the importers lucky enough to get the licenses enjoy the extra $25 in the form of higher prices."

"What determines which importers are the lucky ones?"

"Ah. The fact is, luck has little to do with it. Under a tariff, the government has an extra $25 for every imported television to spend on government programs. Under a quota, the government also has $25 after a fashion in the form of licenses it can distribute to importers. As you might expect, this is not done randomly."

"I assume importers compete in currying favor with government officials to be the beneficiaries of government largesse."

"I assume so as well. Such competition wastes resources from the perspective of the economy as a whole and is an extra cost of a quota. Sometimes the government will give out the licenses to those who have been importers in the past. But even this seemingly innocent choice is likely to be subject to pressure of various kinds."

"How can a quota lead to foreign suppliers capturing the $25 increase in the price of televisions, Dave?"

"This occurs when the government institutes a 'voluntary' quota."

"What's a voluntary quota?"

"A voluntary quota is when a foreign nation agrees 'voluntarily' to restrict its exports to a fixed number. These quotas are sometimes called VERs for 'Voluntary Export Restraints' or VRAs for 'Voluntary Restraint Agreements.' The only thing voluntary about such quotas is the name. An ugly extortionary element comes into play. The United States government tells the Japanese government: 'We would like you to restrict the number of Japanese cars coming into the United States to such-and-such an amount per year.' "

"And if they say no?"

"If they say no, the government can impose a 'real' quota."

"What is the advantage of having the quota seem voluntary?"

"One advantage is that no American politician has to go on record officially supporting a quota. The other advantage is that in principle, it is more flexible. In theory, the American president could ask the Japanese to relax or contract the quota without having to go to Congress. In practice, voluntary quotas are much like a legislated quota. But there is a difference in who captures the profits from higher prices. With a standard, or 'involuntary' quota, U.S. importers control the scarce licenses and make higher profits from the higher prices paid by consumers. With a voluntary quota, the foreign government determines who gets to export the goods to America. The foreign government is given the scarce and valuable rights rather than American importers. As importers compete to get at the scarce supply of foreign goods, the price again gets driven up an additional $25. But now foreigners capture the money."

"Did America ever use voluntary quotas to limit imports, Dave?"

"Not if Frank Bates gets elected in 1960. A Frank Bates election leads to an America of complete self-sufficiency—no imports. That is the world we are in now, where Star looks like it used to and everyone drives a Ford Fairlane or Chevy Impala. In this world, quotas have no meaning because there is nothing to limit."

"But what about the America where Frank Bates is not elected?"

"Then America follows a path of increasingly free trade. That was the world we saw earlier tonight. But even in such a world, American producers were sometimes able to reduce foreign competition using tariffs, quotas, and other means. For example, in 1981, the United States asked the Japanese to limit their exports of cars 'voluntarily.' As you would expect, these limits increased the price of both domestic and imported cars to the American consumer. Economists estimated the effect on the price of an American car from the 'voluntary' restriction of Japanese imports to be at least $400 per car. In 1984, for example, that meant that consumers paid an extra $4 billion to American automakers and their workers because of the restriction on imports. But quotas, voluntary or legislated, had wider effects still."

"For example?"

"Many Japanese auto manufacturers built factories in the United States to get around the limit. This appeared to save American jobs, but it only saved American jobs in the auto industry. If the voluntary quota had been removed and more foreign cars were imported, there would have been an expansion of jobs in those markets producing goods for the Japanese and other nations. Moreover, this would have allowed Americans to specialize in some activities, with the benefits from specialization—increased innovation and performance from increased familiarity with the tasks—the roundabout way to wealth. In addition, there were inefficiencies from the Japanese building a plant in America that might have been better placed in Japan or somewhere else."

"But might not the Japanese want to put a factory in America anyway, to be closer to American customers? They could save transportation costs and gain knowledge of the consumer more easily."

"If such a move made economic sense, they would do so without the quota. Japanese car companies started building car factories in the United States beginning in 1982, the year after the 'voluntary' quota went into effect. Between 1982 and 1990, six Japanese car companies built factories. But cars were just one example of 'voluntary' quotas."

"What was another?"

"There were many. The case of televisions will interest you. Remember when I told you that your American competitors had stopped making televisions?"

"Yes."

"Here is what happened. Zenith saw its profits fall because of foreign competition. This kind of pressure is the reverse of a tariff. As prices charged by foreign competitors fall, American suppliers are forced to lower prices in order to compete. Zenith charged foreign producers with dumping and asked the government to punish their competitors."

"Did they win?"

"They did not, despite the government's flexible definition of what constitutes dumping. But they did get some legislative relief while the case was in progress. The government imposed an 'Orderly Marketing Arrangement.' "

"That's a mouthful."

"It's just a fancy and uninformative name for a voluntary quota. It restricted imports of foreign televisions."

"Did it help?"

"It induced the foreign manufacturers to build assembly plants in the United States to get around the law, as had happened in the automobile industry. That was part of the reason you were able to sell your company to the Japanese in the world of free trade we visited earlier and why they kept the plant outside of Chicago open as an assembly plant. Even when the 'Arrangement' expired, foreign manufacturers continued to build plants here in fear of future 'Arrangements.' Here is the irony. While foreign companies were moving plants to America, Zenith was moving the bulk of its production to Mexico."

"It does sound a bit cockeyed."

"Rather unattractive, wasn't it, Ed? By getting the government to impose a voluntary quota, Zenith forced its competitors to go to the expense of building plants in the United States and using more expensive American workers. Meanwhile, they did much of their production in low-wage Mexico."

"But it didn't work?"

"It did not. Once Zenith lost the dumping case, they were through. The court's decision was applauded by believers in free trade and lampooned as naive by the protectionists. But those protectionists could never explain why the prices of televisions remained low, relative to wages, as we saw when we visited Circuit City."

"What else happens because of quotas, Dave?"

"Energy and initiative, like all commodities, are not in infinite supply. In a world of free trade, American producers are forced to keep up and surpass foreign ingenuity. In a world of restricted trade, producers spend their time trying to lobby the government for ever-wider restrictions. Remember that first trip you made to Washington to see Frank Bates about protection for the television industry? That trip took time and energy. Instead of looking for a better way to make televisions, you lobbied Frank Bates to keep out your competitors. And when you got your way, and Frank Bates passed the bill protecting you and your industry, did the loss of foreign competition change the amount of time you put in trying to improve your product? Tell me, Ed. How did you know that those cars people were driving in the America without imports were Ford Fairlanes?"

"Come on, Dave. I know what a Ford Fairlane looks like."

"Yes, and it looks the same in 2005 as it did in 1960. Wonder why?"

"OK, I get your point. There is less competition. But isn't there a benefit from fewer model changes? You save on design costs and retooling."

"Perhaps. Most consumers like variety. For those who don't, some companies keep their models unchanged for many years. But such savings or losses from less variety are of secondary importance compared to the more important effects. The key change is that without foreign competition, American car manufacturers got lazy and less innovative. The Ford Fairlane is a perfect example."

"But, Dave, it's a pretty good car."

"Yes it is. But we didn't have a chance to look closely at the cars in 2005 when there was free trade. Remember that Honda Accord you were leaning on, back in the parking lot of the movie theater? It had a CD player, an XM satellite radio, and a GPS system with voice recognition. It had—"

"Whoa. Too many letters. Explain."

I explained what a CD player, an XM radio, and a GPS system were. Ed admitted they were all pretty nice.

"Compared to the Fairlane," I continued, "the Honda was structurally safer in a crash even if the air bags and antilock brakes malfunctioned. It could travel almost twice as far on a gallon of gas. It didn't burn oil and it broke down much less often."

"What are air bags and antilock brakes?"

"Safety features that will never be on that Ford Fairlane. When Ford finally designed a car that could compete with the Honda, called the Taurus, it had all the features of the Accord and then some. For a while, it was the best-selling car in America. Do you think Ford would have made the Taurus if the Honda Accord was kept in Japan?"

CHAPTER

Road Trip

I could see that Ed was getting a bit fatigued by his immersion in economics, so I decided to give him a break. A major road trip was in order. We had visited the New Jersey of 2005 twice already, but I had a more scenic and traditional trip planned for Ed, with an ulterior educational motive.

Ed, growing up in Star, hadn't been to the big cities of America too often. So I invited him to take advantage of my powers and visit the tourist attractions of America in the year 2005 when America is free of imports. As we walked together, we only saw American cars on the streets, as it had been in Star. We visited New York, Chicago, Boston, and San Francisco. We saw the Statue of Liberty, the Magnificent Mile, the Freedom Trail, and the Golden Gate Bridge. Then we headed down to Washington, D.C., for the standard tourist attractions: the Washington Monument, the Lincoln Memorial, and the Jefferson Memorial. Ed enjoyed himself immensely.

We sat on a bench on the Mall in Washington, the Washington Monument looming ahead, and Congress behind.

"This is a great country, Dave, even without foreign goods. It makes me so proud."

"It is not my country, but I, too, admire America. Tell me, Ed, did you notice anything unusual about the places we've visited?"

"Not really. I haven't had a chance to visit the tourist attractions of Washington since I was a kid. Too busy making televisions, I guess. They don't seem to have changed as far as I can tell."

"Notice anything unusual about the visitors?"

"Not really. A lot of school kids, as you would expect to see in Washington. Nothing else really grabbed my attention."

"Did you hear any foreign accents while we waited in line?"

"No."

"Did you see any Japanese taking pictures?"

"No."

"Notice any foreign tourists at all?"

"I guess I didn't. Is that unusual?"

"Oh, yes. In the old days, before imports were eliminated, Washington teemed with people from all over the world. The streets of New York would be filled with foreign tourists, both rich and poor. And San Francisco, one of the world's most beautiful cities, would always attract visitors from abroad. But no longer."

"Why not?"

"How does a foreign tourist pay a hotel bill or a restaurant meal?"

"I don't know. Traveler's checks or cash."

"But, Ed, the hotel and restaurant will only accept American currency. How would people in Tokyo get dollars? Or people in France? Or England? Or Germany?"

"They would go to their bank and—"

"But where would that bank get dollars, Ed? A bank has dollars only if there are Americans willing to swap dollars for francs, yen, or pounds. If no foreign goods are allowed into the country, then Americans are not spending dollars on exports. With no money spent on exports, foreign banks have no dollars to swap for the domestic currencies of their own country."

"I never thought of tourism that way."

"The purchases of a tourist in America are really the same as exports. When a foreign tourist spends a night in a New York hotel, it is the same as shipping goods abroad without paying a transportation fee. It is the same with a restaurant meal. A restaurant meal eaten by a foreign tourist is the same as shipping food abroad. A foreign tourist's expenditures are a way to export goods and services in a funny way. Instead of shipping the food there, the foreigner comes and picks it up here. The tourist pays the freight charge."

"The concept of exporting services is a strange one."

"Yes, but potentially very important. An extraordinary example of such an export is university education. America has the best universities in the world, and under free trade foreign students come to America to enjoy that service. Without trade, those students don't have the dollars to spend on American education. At Washington University in St. Louis, where your daughter Susan earned her MBA—"

"Susan has an MBA?"

"She does. And the business school at Washington University has a lot of students from overseas. In fact, Susan was the president of a student club for international business. She brought speakers in from Japan and even spent the summer between her first and second year of classes in a summer internship in Hong Kong."

"Susan spent a summer in Hong Kong?"

"She did in the world of free trade. Without free trade, well—"

"Well?"

"Be patient. We'll see Susan soon. The point is that foreign students enriched Susan's view of the world and opened her eyes beyond the Midwest until she could see beyond the Pacific. That's why she ended up working for Mast Industries and The Limited under free trade. You can imagine how studying together with foreign students makes the world a cozier place. And how tourists to and from America build ties between nations."

"Are there no tourists visiting America? Are no Americans visiting foreign countries?"

"There are a few. Americans who can afford to travel supply a handful of dollars while they are abroad that form a pool of American money for tourists who wish to visit here. But the government had to limit the number of foreign visitors and immigrants as well, even if they could have acquired dollars."

"Why would the government do that?"

"Smuggling. When you ban foreign imports, quality declines and price increases. Goods get more expensive. This creates a black market in imports. Foreigners would come to America pretending to be tourists. Their real goal was to swap their cheaper foreign goods to Americans for dollars to pay for American goods."

"Come on, Dave. How much stuff could people bring in as tourists?"

"A lot more than you can imagine. A lot of goods came over the Mexican and Canadian borders. Boats landed at night all along the American coastline. People would smuggle the goods in and use the dollars to buy American goods or to enjoy American life for a while as a tourist. You have to remember the profits available. Don't you think it would be worthwhile to try and smuggle coffee into America? Or shirts by wearing a few extra? Or diamonds? The government had to put a lot of people to work to help stop the smuggling. To save costs, they put a lot of restrictions on legal entry into the United States. So there aren't a lot of tourists, and not many Americans have any foreign currency to take abroad. So Americans take a lot of trips to Washington."

"It's sad."

"Yes, it is. A lot of hotels and restaurants went out of business."

"And there is a lot less communication between people. That can't be healthy."

"No, I don't think so either. You're lucky I made it through customs. Special visa."

We sat in silence and looked out over the panorama of monuments that make up the Washington skyline. I had an idea.

"Ed, let's make one more stop before we get back to business."

"Sure. Where to?"

"Close your eyes. Now open them."

"We're in England, Dave! There's a real English pub! I've always dreamed of having a beer in an English pub. Is there some way we can have a drink in there despite our unreal existence?"

"Go and see. Ask for yourself."

"Money is going to be a bit of problem. I've only got a few American coins. But, Dave, it would make sense for you to have a few pounds on you. Can we do it?"

"I'm afraid finance is not my line anymore. But we shall see what develops. 'Belly up to the bar,' as the expression goes. Let's see what happens."

We headed inside.

"The place is deserted, Dave. There's no one here. The taps are dry."

"I'm sorry to disappoint you, Ed."

"This place gives me the creeps. Are we in some London slum?"

"Let's go outside and look around. Perhaps we can get our bearings."

We wandered back out into bright sunlight. We were on a winding cobblestoned street, then suddenly a clearing.

"Where have you brought me, Dave? What's that funny structure across the lagoon there?"

"That is a bit of the Eiffel Tower."

"But that's in France, Dave. And what are those other strange buildings? They're all falling down. Is that a pagoda?"

"This is what was known as Epcot Center, Ed. Built by the Walt Disney Company, it was an incredible tourist attraction. Tourists came from all over the world and America to enjoy it. This part was called the World Showcase. Nations of the world built pavilions to capture the flavor of their countries. There were movies on screens that surrounded you, extraordinary displays of a nation's heritage, art, food, and drink. When America stopped trading with the rest of the world, the foreign tourists stopped coming. At first, Epcot had a bit of a renaissance. Americans couldn't go abroad so they came here to satisfy their thirst for things foreign. But Disney eventually lost so much money that they shut it down. No one cares about it anymore. It's falling apart."

"It makes my skin crawl."

"You should have been here when the sun sparkled on the lake. In front of the Japanese pavilion, a Japanese artist blew what looked like glass into the shapes of animals and fish. As each delicate piece was completed, he would give them to the mesmerized children gathered around him. Only it was not glass, but spun sugar. What a delicious dilemma for a child. There was street theater here in these English streets, and, yes, the warm English beer flowed. I tell you—"

"Please stop, Dave. Take us back to Star."

"As you wish."

CHAPTER

10

The Case for Protection

We were back in Star. And Ed was still troubled.

"You make it out to be so black and white, Dave. Maybe tariffs and quotas don't produce jobs. But there are other reasons for protecting some industries from foreign competition."

"For example?"

"National security. America doesn't want to be dependent on foreigners for anything with military significance. They could blackmail us."

"What type of product is vital in times of war?"

"Steel."

"Steel is not as essential as it once was. Titanium is more critical. But let's consider steel because America's steel producers never seem to tire of asking for protection. But even if America's security depended on steel, keeping out cheap foreign steel isn't necessary if steel comes from many different nations, and some of them are allies. It is hard to imagine that all steel producers will be America's enemies in time of war. Even so, what size steel industry do you think is necessary to be a springboard for wartime production? In World War II America was able to increase its steel production enormously under wartime mobilization. I think America could do it again very quickly. In the meanwhile, America would have the enormous stock of planes and tanks she has already amassed."

"Dave, are you admitting that a tariff on steel might be justifiable if our steel came from enemies we might fight in a war?"

"Sure, in theory, under that unlikely condition. In practice, it might be wiser to create either a public or private strategic reserve to avoid the threat of blackmail. But you can be sure that business people in many industries will do all they can to convince people that their product is vital for national security."

"What about a case for protection when an industry is just starting out? Without protection, it will be destroyed by foreign competition. When the industry matures, tariffs or quotas can be removed."

"Ah, the infant-industry argument. Virtually all businesses and industries lose money at the start. That is what an investment is all about. You give up money today for a greater sum tomorrow. Either the money you make later is enough to compensate for the amount you lose at the start, or it is not. If it is great enough, then you do not need protection. If the money you make later does not make up for the initial losses, then protection is a mistake. You are protecting an investment that never should have been made in the first place."

"But what if foreign competitors lower their prices to make those initial losses unbearable? Without the help of a tariff to make things fair, how are they going to get started?"

"Ed, it is a theoretical possibility that foreign competitors would squash an American upstart. Even this possibility requires foreign competitors to be willing to sustain the massive losses necessary to absorb all of the demand for their product that low prices produce. If they do not, the American competitor will be able to sell its output at a higher price. Where is the evidence that it has ever occurred? When did an American industry begin production only to give up in the face of cutthroat pricing by foreign competitors, followed by an increase in price by those foreign competitors? For this argument to be sustained empirically, you have to make a completely untestable, unverifiable claim."

"Yes, Dave?"

"You have to claim that the threat of foreign competition is so insidious, so conspiratorial, and so effective, that American companies never came into existence in the first place. I find this argument uncompelling."

"Are there any other arguments in favor of protection?"

"There is no end to the creativity of business in finding arguments for government assistance. As Milton Friedman has pointed out, every businessman favors free markets while arguing that his own industry has special circumstances justifying government intervention in the national interest. But even academic economists sometimes make at least a theoretical case in favor of protection."

"Let's hear one."

"Consider a large country such as the United States, whose demand for a product makes up a substantial part of the world market."

"Say for televisions."

"Correct, at least at certain times. The argument for protection goes like this: If America is a large demander of televisions, then a tariff that reduces the demand for televisions by the Americans can actually reduce the price of televisions."

"A tax reduces the price?"

"Not the full price to the consumer including the tariff. That still rises. But the price of the television before the tariff is added on can actually go down. Suppose again that televisions are selling initially for $250. A $25 tariff will typically increase the price to $275. This assumes that the prices of televisions in other parts of the world are unaffected and stay at $250. Because they stay at $250 everywhere else in the world, the price in America must go to $275 when the tariff of $25 is put on. Otherwise, foreign sellers would not be willing to bring a television into America."

"Makes sense."

"But the price will not jump the full amount of the tariff if the United States has a sufficiently large share of the world television market. In this case, when America puts a tariff in place, American sales still go down. But this reduction is a significant reduction in worldwide sales, because we are assuming the United States is a large part of the world market. Foreign producers will try to sell the televisions they used to sell in America elsewhere. In the case where the United States is a small part of the world market, it is easy to sell those televisions somewhere else without lowering the price. But if the lost sales in the United States are a large part of the world market, they will have to lower their price in order to sell the same number of televisions they did before. Televisions around the world become less expensive. The overall decrease in the world demand for televisions caused by the reduction in the size of the American market could lower the price of televisions to, say, $240. When you add in the $25 tariff, the price goes to only $265 instead of $275."

"But aren't consumers still going to be worse off?"

"Yes. Consumers will be worse off by $15, but America will have $25 of revenue from the tariff on each television. So there is a net gain to the United States of $10 per television. Essentially, the United States has acted like a cartel of customers rather than the typical case where there is a cartel of sellers. A cartel of sellers withholds supply to get a higher price. In this case, the United States withholds demand to get a lower price."

"Sounds pretty good."

"Its attractiveness is what motivated a great economist, Francis Edgeworth, to say that this argument in favor of tariffs should be put in the medicine chest but labeled 'Poison.'"

"Why, Dave?"

"While theoretically beneficial, in practice there is no guarantee that the benefits will come to pass."

"Why not?"

"Many reasons. You may think you can affect the world price of televisions, when in fact your impact is negligible. Most countries, even the United States, make a trivial contribution to the world demand for any product."

"But if demand is reduced from one country, isn't the price around the world going to fall at least a small amount?"

"Probably not. Suppose you think the price of apples is too high, and you stop eating apples. What happens to the price of apples in the supermarket?"

"Nothing."

"Exactly. And the reason is that in the world market for apples, taking out your demand has an insignificant effect on the world apple market. Now suppose every citizen of the state of Illinois stopped eating apples. What is the effect on the price of apples?"

"I give up."

"The answer again is nothing. The citizens of Illinois make up such a small part of the apple market that removing their demand has a negligible effect on price."

"But, Dave, if Americans stopped eating apples, wouldn't the price go down?"

"Probably. But I will give you an example to suggest otherwise. Do you know that the American government borrows money to help finance government activity?"

"Sure, and it makes me plenty nervous. Our national debt is way too big."

"I've got news for you, Ed. It's going to get a lot bigger. In fact, there were years after 1960 when the American government borrowed over $400 billion dollars."

"That must have plunged the country into a depression!"

"Why, Ed?"

"Because to get people to buy the bonds, interest rates would go sky high, and no private investment will take place."

"That's what people said. Yet interest rates were quite low when U.S. government borrowing was high."

"How could that be?"

"Because even though $400 billion seems like a lot of money, it is not so large when seen in the context of the world market for borrowing. The United States borrowed that money, and interest rates hardly moved at all. For the same reason, a tariff on televisions coming into America that lowers American demand for televisions, and thus world demand, may leave the price around the world unchanged at $250."

"But in the case where America's demand is large enough to affect the world demand for a product, then wouldn't a tariff be good for the United States?"

"Not so fast. Even in that case, you must have great confidence in the government. The government has to be good at two things. First, it has to be good at estimating the effect of the tariff on the world price. What if they pick a tariff that is too large? A large tariff raises the price dramatically to the U.S. consumer, causing a large reduction in U.S. and, consequently, world demand. The price of televisions will fall, and the government will have the tariff revenue. But consumers are paying higher prices and enjoying fewer televisions. They are harmed. If you make the tariff too big, that harm can outweigh the gains to other Americans from the tariff revenue."

"That should be easy to prevent. Just make sure that the tariff is not too big."

"That sounds easy. But even if you pick a 'small' tariff, if the effect of the tariff on demand in the United States is sufficiently large, you can have an equally disastrous effect."

"So just make sure that you anticipate the effect of the tariff."

"That is not so easy to do. But to make matters worse, guess who has an incentive to make sure the tariff is set at a high level?"

"The domestic producer of televisions, someone like myself?"

"Exactly. The domestic producer will be talking constantly about how important it is for the United States to set a large tariff and take advantage of this opportunity to generate revenue from foreigners."

"OK, so watch out for lobbyists."

"Alas, that is not the only problem."

"What else?"

"You have to make sure that the government spends the $25 it has collected from each television wisely. Otherwise, the net gain to the United States disappears."

"But if the United States is a large enough demander of the product, and if the tariff is set at the right level, and if the government spends the money wisely, then a tariff can have a beneficial effect?"

"Yes. Except for one small detail."

"I have a suspicion that you are being sarcastic about the size of the detail, Dave."

"I apologize. You are correct. It is no small detail. The preceding argument assumes that the rest of the world does nothing when the United States puts a tariff on their goods. There is nothing to stop a foreign producer from retaliating with tariffs on American goods. Even if the initial tariff in America is set carefully, the retaliation can leave America worse off than before."

"So even though there is an argument in favor of a tariff when a country's demand for a product is a significant portion of world demand, you are saying that it can backfire. Are there any other arguments by academics for protection?"

"Some academics promote the idea of strategic trade policy. They argue that there are some industries that are sufficiently crucial that the government should help them, particularly to make sure that they are the first entrant into the marketplace."

"It is important to be the first into a market."

"Sometimes. Sometimes it is better to be second. Or, more accurately, sometimes it is no handicap not to be the first. But it is conceivable that for certain industries or products, it is good to be first."

"What does that have to do with protection?"

"Suppose two countries have companies vying to be the first to bring a technology to market. Then you could argue that the government should subsidize its own domestic firm and punish the foreign firm with protection. That way, the domestic firm gets a large market share early in the battle. In particular, the argument is made that because high-technology products lead to many other products, then America should make sure to maintain its edge in high-technology products lest other nations come to dominate those markets and enjoy the products that flow from the technology. This would be particularly true for high-technology products that may have room in the world market for only one supplier."

"Sounds pretty reasonable. Is this a legitimate argument for a government role in international competition?"

"Perhaps."

"But?"

"There are many questions to be asked. How do you know whether a high-technology product will have many 'spin-offs,' as they are called? How do you know when there will be room for only one supplier? Can you think of many examples? Are you sure that being first is such an advantage? Might it not be better to see how the product fares? And, finally, when government is handing out money and favors, how can you be sure that government will choose the right products to protect? Political influence may play a larger role than concern for the overall well-being of the people."

"OK. Are there answers to those questions?"

"Based on economic theory, no; so I would again encourage empirical observation. For example, in the 1970s the French and British governments teamed up to produce an enormous technological breakthrough called the supersonic transport, or SST. This was a plane designed to fly from New York to London at a speed you will have difficulty comprehending."

"I can't say I've ever flown to London."

"At the time the plane was under design, the standard jet made the trip in about seven hours. The fruit of the SST project was a plane called the Concorde. The Concorde could make the trip in three and a half hours."

"That sounds pretty fabulous, Dave. Think of the savings in time and productivity for people trying to do business in both London and New York. The Concorde sounds like a case where government-sponsored technology paid off."

"In one sense, it is a textbook case of the sort of market we are describing. The market for people who wish to travel from New York to London in three and a half hours is a relatively small one. The Concorde, perhaps by being first, had the market all to itself."

"A monopoly?"

"In a sense. There was competition from the flights taking the full seven hours. But if you wanted to get to London or New York quickly, you had to fly the Concorde or know a dead British economist on a mission to save his soul."

"So how about it, Dave. Was the Concorde a winner?"

"Only for the people who traveled on it. For the investors, the British and French taxpayers, it was an unmitigated disaster."

"But they had a monopoly on the market."

"Yes. But the market was too small at the prices the Concorde had to charge to cover its costs. Yes, the Concorde had a monopoly; and yes, the British and the French implemented the technology before anyone else. Unfortunately, it was a very bad investment. Being first has its rewards, but they must be sufficiently large to outweigh the costs, or your investment is a poor one."

"How bad an investment was it?"

"The plane was conceived in 1962 but didn't fly until 1976. The investment by 1976 was $4.3 billion. By 1983, revenues covered operating costs, but given the losses in the preceding years, there is no way the investment paid off. They would have been better off putting their money in a savings account. Finally, in 2003, they simply gave up. The Concorde was grounded. You can find it in a museum but it no longer flies."

"I see your point, but it's just one example."

"Let me give you another. But first, note a deeper flaw in the Concorde. The money from the Concorde came from the taxpayers of Britain and France. They implicitly made the investment and came out on the short end. What do you think is the profile of the typical taxpayer in those countries?"

"I don't know."

"Nor do I. But the typical taxpayer is somewhere in the middle class. Who do you think is the typical traveler on the Concorde?"

"Not a middle-class French or British taxpayer."

"Bravo, Ed. The fare from New York to London and back on the Concorde in 1999 was over $10,000, as much as seven times the cost on slower planes. Only the wealthiest of the wealthy find their time sufficiently valuable or the novelty of the Concorde sufficiently high to pay the premium. The fare did not cover the true cost of the trip. The correct price should have included a return for the earlier research and development as well as the operating costs. The average taxpayer was subsidizing the wealthy traveler."

"They could fix that, couldn't they, Dave?"

"How?"

"By putting a tax on the traveler. And using the revenue to help the taxpayer."

"Another roundabout idea from our conversation. Interesting. Of course price accomplishes exactly the same thing in a private enterprise."

"How is that?"

"Why didn't private companies invest in the Concorde technology on their own? Why did it take the government's subsidies to make the investment profitable? Without the government subsidies, the project was not profitable. What does it mean to say that a project is not profitable? It means that the price one expects to be able to charge is not high enough to cover the costs of the project. When the price is high enough to cover the costs, the users of the good pay for the benefits they enjoy, not some third party who is forced to contribute."

"But if the costs could not be covered by the price, why did the British and French government enter into the project?"

"The cynical explanation is that the governments paid more attention to the demands of their aerospace companies than to the costs and benefits accruing to the nation as a whole. The more charitable explanation is that either their estimate of the costs and expected fares differed from the estimates of private companies, or the governments hoped for the national advantage that technology supposedly yields."

"Why would the governments estimate the costs and expected price so poorly?"

"What is their incentive to do so accurately? They have no stockholders to face, only taxpayers. Taxpayers tend to have fewer places to turn than investors in a private company."

"Did any of those technological benefits come to pass?"

"Not that the eye can see. In fact, as should be clear to you now, the net effect of this project was to make the people of Britain and France poorer. Some individuals benefited, as is always the case in these examples. But the net effect on the citizenry was negative."

"But surely some government investments in technology paid off, Dave."

"There were some happier endings than the Concorde. European countries subsidized the creation of Airbus, a producer of more conventional airplanes, which were slower than the Concorde but more profitable."

"So Airbus was a good investment for the people of Europe?"

"That is a harder question to answer. Airbus guaranteed a European competitor to Boeing and McDonnell Douglas."

"That was good for Europe, wasn't it?"

"Competition in the aircraft business is good for almost everybody. But few of the alleged benefits from technology investments flowed from the Airbus subsidies. The main impact was to keep some aircraft assembly jobs in Europe."

"But the competition kept the prices down for new aircraft, didn't it, Dave?"

"Sure. But the competition would have probably been there without Airbus. When Airbus thrived, McDonnell Douglas struggled and eventually got purchased by Boeing. By the year 2000, there were only two major suppliers of new, large passenger aircraft: Boeing and Airbus. If Airbus hadn't been subsidized, there would probably still be two competitors. One of them would have been McDonnell Douglas instead of Airbus. America would have had a few more thousand aircraft assembly jobs and Europe a few thousand fewer. It's hard to know what kind of return the taxpayers of

Europe got on the investment of those subsidies. But it's hard to argue that making airplanes is a key to a nation's prosperity. A better case could be made for computers. In the late 1980s, Americans were concerned that America might lose its dominance in semiconductors, or computer chips, to the Japanese. You may remember that semiconductors are the guts that make computers what they are."

"And did the American government help the semiconductor industry?"

"A little bit. The government started a research institute called Sematech and subsidized half of the costs, about $100 million each year. The rest was paid for by participating companies. The American government also tried to open up the Japanese market to American suppliers of chips."

"Did it work?"

"Encouraging the Japanese to buy American chips hurt the computer business. American chips were more expensive at first, so computers got more expensive. By the end of the 1990s, American firms, particularly one called Intel, dominated the industry again. Eventually, American-made chips got dramatically cheaper."

"Did Sematech help?"

"Probably not. Their efforts were small compared to the privately funded research and development. Rather than augment total research and development, Sematech seems to have had very little impact—firms cut back on some of their basic research because they saw that Sematech was doing it. By the end of the 1990s, Sematech allowed foreign members to join. It was no longer a tool of American industrial policy."

"But it may have served a purpose."

"Perhaps. It was never large enough to be a serious experiment in what advocates called 'Industrial Policy' or 'Strategic Trade Policy.' Those ideas lost credence in the late 1990s when Japan, the country most known for government support of key industries and technologies, went into a prolonged economic slump. They will recover eventually. But it will take a while before the idea of industrial policy or strategic policy recovers. There is just too much potential for mistakes like the Concorde; or worse, the potential for abuse of government by special interests—companies who want to use a theoretical case for protection to justify helping a narrower interest than the country as a whole."

"I don't know, Dave. It seems to me that new technologies are a special case because of the risk involved."

"New technology is inherently risky, Ed. Who bears that risk most effectively, the company and its stockholders, or the taxpayer?"

"There must be times you can make the case for the taxpayer. America as a whole gets many of the benefits, Dave."

"But America as a whole gets those benefits in most cases even if, say, the French get the technology first. American consumers still get the product. America might not get the jobs in that industry. But what is to stop America from entering the industry once it gets started?"

"You gave the answer yourself. What if there is only room for one firm? Isn't it better for America if that one firm is American?"

"It will be better for the workers in that one firm. Not much of a case can be made that it is better for Americans in general. Besides, I await a real-world example of this one firm that is so often discussed. The only case I know of is the Concorde. France and Britain together controlled the market for quick trips around the world. This market supremacy did not lead to great wealth for France or Britain. You would be hard pressed to find another case where the market for a technology was so narrow that there was only room for a single producer and where government intervention would determine which firm got in the market first. But companies keep arguing for protection from foreign competition and government subsidies in the name of the public good."

"They might have tariffs or quotas. Or they might have other barriers to imports that were harder to observe."

"OK. So how would you know if overall they were treating American products fairly?"

"I don't know. I'd look at the overall trade patterns between the two nations."

"If you and I are going to discuss the issue of fair trade, we have to consider a world where America imports something. In 2005, for example, in the America without a Frank Bates presidency, America ran a trade deficit in goods and services of $200 billion with China. America's—

"Two hundred billion? One country exports $200 billion more in goods and services than it imports from us? That's almost half the size of the U.S. economy, Dave!"

CHAPTER

Do Trade Deficits Hurt America?

"**B**ut, Dave, what about the argument for a level playing field? If the other guys won't let our products into their countries, why should we let their products into ours?"

"If your enemy cut off his nose, would you cut yours off out of fairness?"

"What?"

"If foreign nations keep out American products, they are harming themselves. They are forcing their citizens to pay higher prices than necessary for the goods they consume. They are devoting unnecessary resources, people, raw materials, and capital to produce goods they could import at a lower cost. Should America impose the same costs on its citizens?"

"No, but it still isn't fair. If we're going to let foreign companies sell here, they should let American companies sell there."

"I would call it misguided rather than unfair. But let me ask you first, how would you know if a foreign nation is keeping out American goods or services?"

"They might have tariffs or quotas. Or they might have other barriers to imports that were harder to observe."

"OK. So how would you know if, overall, they were treating American products fairly?"

"I don't know. I'd look at the overall trade patterns between the two nations."

"If you and I are going to discuss the issue of fair trade, we have to consider a world where America imports something. In 2005, for example, in the America without a Frank Bates presidency, America ran a trade deficit in goods and services of $200 billion with China. America's—"

"Two hundred billion! One country exports $200 billion more in goods and services than it imports from us? That's almost half the size of the U.S. economy, Dave!"

"It would be if the economy were the same size in 2005 and 1960. GDP in 1960 was about $500 billion. In 2005, in a world of trade, it was $12 trillion. So $200 billion doesn't look quite as large. Overall, America's trade deficit in goods and services in 2005 was $726 billion."

"How can you be so nonchalant about a number that big? That's almost a trillion dollars! Doesn't that prove my point? Something unfair must have been going on."

"Perhaps. How many oranges does Minnesota import from Florida in a given year?"

"I don't know. A lot."

"How many oranges do you think Florida imports from Minnesota?"

"Zero."

"Isn't that unfair, Ed? Shouldn't Florida help out Minnesota by importing just as many oranges from Minnesota as Minnesota imports from Florida?"

"But that doesn't make any sense, Dave. Minnesota doesn't produce any oranges."

"But they could, you know. They could build greenhouses, heat them year-round if necessary, and have a huge orange crop. Of course, Minnesota oranges would be very expensive. One suspects the citizens of Florida would rather eat their home-grown oranges at a lower price. But that wouldn't stop the orange producers of Minnesota from demanding that Floridians eat Minnesota oranges in the name of fairness. Or worse, that the producers of Florida oranges use air conditioning in their fields to make sure that there was a level playing field for the orange producers in both states."

"That's a misleading example, Dave. You can't look at just one product."

"No, but the example shows the foolishness of looking at unequal trade flows as inherently unfair. Trade flows should be unequal. My point is that if you pick any one state in the United States and look at its trade position with respect to other states, you'd see a lot of deficits and surpluses. But there are no trade barriers between the states. So those deficits and surpluses wouldn't tell you anything about whether a state's products are being treated fairly. The same holds internationally. It would make no sense for the United States to have equal trade flows with every country for every good. The essence of trade is specialization."

"But if we import more from the rest of the world than they import from us by $726 billion, then the nations of the world must be treating our products unfairly in some general sense. Otherwise, our imports would match our exports."

"Let's see. Back in Star, you like to shop at that little corner grocery near your house run by Howard Wilkinson, right?"

"That's right, Dave, and he's a fine man, except for one thing. He—"

"He doesn't own a Stellar television."

"That's right! You're amazing, Dave."

"It's nothing. So why doesn't he?"

"He claims his wife doesn't like the color of our cabinets. She says the color clashes with the décor of her den, so she owns one from the competition. It drives me crazy."

"But you still shop at his grocery."

"Oh sure. He's got the best produce in town."

"So you run a trade deficit with Howard. You buy more from him than he buys from you. Even if he bought one of your televisions every once in a while, you'd still run a deficit because your grocery bill is greater than his television budget, right?

"That's true."

"Ever lose any sleep over the fact that you spend more with him than he spends with you?"

"No."

"And here's the funny thing. You don't really run a deficit with Howard. Oh, you run a trade deficit, all right. You buy more goods from him than he buys from you. But your overall relationship with Howard is balanced."

"How's that?"

"He gives you $100 or so worth of groceries every month and you give him $100 worth of goods. But instead of giving him $100 worth of televisions, you give him currency. That lets him take $100 worth of goods from you by reducing your bank account and buying what he wants."

"What's that have to do with America?"

"Americans and foreigners don't just trade goods, they trade assets and currency as well. When America imports from the rest of the world, foreigners could take the dollars they get and buy American goods. But there are other things they do with dollars. Sometimes they just hold them."

"Well, that can't be good. It doesn't stimulate our economy."

"Ed, when your wife shops at Howard's, she pays with a check, doesn't she?"

"Sure."

"What if Howard decided not to cash your checks because he thought they were pretty? Suppose he decided to frame each of them and put them on the wall of his office."

"I'd say he'd gone crazy."

"No doubt. But would it hurt your family's finances if he told you that from now on, he wanted to keep your checks uncashed?"

"No. It sounds pretty good. It sounds like free groceries."

"Exactly! And if he didn't cash your checks, do you think it would hurt the economy of Star?"

"Of course not, Dave. If Howard didn't cash our checks that would just free up money we could spend on other things."

"Aha! It's the same with the United States. When Americans buy goods from foreigners, those green pieces of paper the foreigners receive in return are claims on American goods and services. If instead of spending the pieces of paper, foreigners decide to hold them, then that means more goods and services for Americans to enjoy. It is the closest thing to a free lunch that an economist can imagine. Of course, while some foreigners do spend the money, it isn't always on goods and services, which is why America often runs a trade deficit with the rest of the world."

"But I'm confused, Dave. Why wouldn't they find American goods appealing?"

"They do. But sometimes they prefer American assets, such as shares of stock, bonds, land, or buildings."

"But aren't those purchases included in the trade balance?"

"No. They are accounted for separately in what is called the capital account. So when America is running a trade deficit, it is almost always running a capital account surplus. A capital account surplus means that foreigners buy more American assets as investments than Americans buy of foreign assets. And if that's true, America will run a deficit in goods with respect to the rest of the world."

"So does the capital surplus make up for the trade deficit?"

"In accounting terms, yes, when you include the currency that flows between countries. But I assume you're curious about whether it's good for America."

"Yes."

"The simple answer is that focusing on one account or the other is a red herring. There is no simple cause of one or the other, but the two move together in response to a myriad of decisions by millions of individuals about how much to save, where to invest, and what goods to buy. For example, it is tempting to say that America runs a trade deficit because foreign nations won't let their citizens buy American products. But as long as foreigners want to buy more American assets than Americans wish to buy foreign assets, America will run a trade deficit even if every country in the world was free of all trade barriers and welcomed American products as freely as their own. If America is a great place to invest relative to the rest of the world, and if foreigners save a sufficient amount relative to Americans, America will run a trade deficit."

"But can America continue to run a trade deficit year after year?"

"A lot of people worried about that because they claimed that America's trade deficit was being financed by borrowing—by debt. And debt means living beyond your means and, as we all know, you can't live beyond your means forever. There's a day of reckoning."

"That does sound bad."

"Perhaps, but it simply wasn't true. Yes, some of the Americans assets that foreigners bought were government bonds to finance spending by the American government. But the bulk of the assets weren't government debt. They were real estate and stocks issued by American companies interested in expanding and innovating. Some of the assets were corporate bonds, but that was a way for American corporations to finance new activity, not as a way to live beyond their means. The capital surplus was actually a sign of strength, a sign that American assets were good investments relative to risks in the rest of the world."

"But what if foreign holders of U.S assets or U.S. bonds suddenly decided to sell off their investments? Wouldn't that damage the United States? Wasn't that a threat to American prosperity?"

"But why would foreigners suddenly be eager to sell assets they once found attractive? Only some unforeseen turn of events in the United States that would signal to investors that their investments were at risk could be the cause. But then the selling of assets would be an effect rather than a cause of economic problems. And who would buy those assets during that fire sale? The prices would fall dramatically and the foreign sellers would be the ones who were punished. It wouldn't hurt Americans."

"OK, Dave. But it still makes me nervous to have foreigners buying up American assets and controlling them."

"You're not alone. In the 1980s, in a world where America is open to trade, foreigners bought a lot of American assets—real estate, government bonds, and shares in American companies. People were particularly worried about the Japanese. They were afraid the Japanese would be able to manipulate these assets to harm Americans or steal the profits. For example, the Japanese bought the Algonquin Hotel in New York. It was something of a cultural landmark because a group of intellectuals of the 1930s used to gather there for drinks and try to impress each other with witty remarks."

"And what did the Japanese do with the hotel?"

"They tore it down and left an eyesore in midtown Manhattan to punish the American people and reduce real-estate values in the surrounding area."

"Aha!"

"Just kidding, Ed. Strangely enough, after paying an enormous sum for the property, they wanted to run it as profitably as possible. They did not turn it into the world's largest sushi restaurant or—"

"What's sushi?"

"Raw fish."

"Thank goodness for that decision."

"People were afraid they would create a super-modern high-technology atrocity that would appeal to Japanese tastes. Instead they decided to restore the hotel to its grandeur of the 1930s. That was the most profitable use of the asset."

"I can see why people were worried about Japanese purchases of American assets. The Japanese earn all of the profits instead of the Americans who owned it before."

"That appears to be the case. But the exact opposite turns out to be true."

"Come on, Dave. If the Japanese own it, they get the profits. What could be more straightforward than that?"

"I don't know, Ed. I would have thought that after a few lessons in the roundabout way that you would be wary of 'straightforward' reasoning."

"I may not be used to roundabout reasoning, but I am getting used to being wrong. Let's hear it."

"Suppose you had a money tree."

"A money tree?"

"Yes, a tree that every year produced a beautiful harvest of money. If it will make the example easier to understand, think of an apple tree. After all, an apple tree is a money tree; you just have to go to the trouble of selling the fruit in order to turn it into money."

"OK."

"So you have a money tree. A \$20-bill tree. Every year this money tree has about five \$20 bills that ripen on it, for a total of \$100. Of course, some years it rains more than other years, and you get six bills. In the bad years, you might get four. But on average, the tree produces five bills for a total of \$100. One day you decide to sell the tree. What would your asking price be?"

"I don't know, Dave. I don't know much about the money-tree market."

"But you do. Let's reverse your position. Suppose you wanted to buy such a tree. How much would you be willing to pay for it?"

"Does the tree live and grow forever?"

"An excellent question. Let us suppose the tree lives for 10 years and dies."

"Then I suppose the most I would pay for it would be \$1,000."

"Why?"

"If the tree produces \$100 per year for 10 years, that's \$1,000. If I could buy the tree for less than \$1,000, I would make a profit. I would never pay more than \$1,000 unless I liked looking at money trees."

"You are close to the right answer. You would certainly never pay more than \$1,000. But if you think for another minute, you would not pay even close to \$1,000. Your choice is to buy the tree or not buy the tree. Suppose the price is \$1,000. If you do not buy the tree, you get to keep your \$1,000. If you buy the tree, you can expect to earn \$100 per year for 10 years. Is \$100 per year for 10 years equal to \$1,000?"

"Of course not. I see that now. One hundred dollars per year for 10 years is worth less than \$1,000. Rather than investing my \$1,000 in the money tree, I could invest it and earn interest. At the end of 10 years, I would have my principal of \$1,000 intact, plus I would have earned a lot of interest along the way. So, if the money tree is priced at $1,000, it is a bad buy."

"Exactly. A money tree such as the one I have described will have to sell for something less than $1,000. How much less depends on the rate of interest a person can expect to earn in alternative investments of equal risk."

"Fine. That's very interesting, Dave. But what does that have to do with the Algonquin Hotel?"

"The Algonquin Hotel, like every form of capital, is in essence a money tree. It provides a stream of income for a period of years, just like the tree. The selling price of such an asset depends on its future profitability. The American who puts the Algonquin up for sale will demand and be able to receive a price that is approximately equal to the sum of all the future profits of the hotel. It will actually be less than that because while the buyer waits to receive the future profits, the seller has the freedom to enjoy the money now."

"Are you trying to tell me that when the Algonquin is making profits under Japanese ownership, that money is already in the pockets of the American who sold the hotel?"

"That's right. If there were no uncertainty, the profits earned by the new Japanese owners would be just canceled by the amount the American owners received when they sold the property plus the interest earned on the money in the meanwhile. Do you know what actually happened? Remember that the harvest of any money tree is in fact uncertain. In the 1980s, the Japanese paid a lot of money for a number of assets that were particularly renowned. They bought the Pebble Beach Golf Links, Rockefeller Center, and other such properties. For better or worse, those properties turned out to be far less profitable than the selling price predicted. So the Japanese overpaid their American sellers. It looked as if the Japanese were earning profits. In fact, on balance, the American sellers profited."

"So it was OK that we sold all those assets to the Japanese because they overpaid?"

"No, that was just a twist of fate I was pointing out. The real point is that who owns something isn't that important, as long as they use it wisely. Why should an American care if a Japanese or a Chinese or a British or Dutch investor offers more than an American for a share in an American company? America benefits from foreign capital. It means America has more resources to use for creativity and innovation."

"Still, Dave, I can understand that some Americans disliked the idea of the Japanese owning Rockefeller Center. It's such an American spot. I once took Steven and Susan ice skating there."

"I think the American selling Rockefeller Center was very eager to allow the highest bidder, foreign or American, to be allowed to buy the property. And when the Japanese owned it, they still made sure to keep the ice good and frozen. And when America raised the biggest outcry against Japanese ownership, in the 1980s, Japan was sometimes only the third-largest investor in American assets, behind England and Holland. No one felt uncomfortable about English or Dutch purchases. Makes you wonder, doesn't it?"

"OK, Dave, but just because trade deficits are the flip side of capital surpluses, that doesn't mean they're harmless. Wouldn't it be better to run a trade surplus and a capital-account deficit?"

"Why is that, Ed?"

"If we could balance our trade or get to a surplus, wouldn't that mean more exports for America, more demand for American products, and more jobs?"

"I am not going to answer that question."

"Too easy?"

"Yes. Think about it for a moment."

"I guess I think like a businessman, Dave, not like an economist. Let me see. Increasing exports increases jobs only in the export industries. The old roundabout way to wealth. It wouldn't mean more jobs overall."

"Excellent, Dave. But opponents of free trade always argued that trade deficits destroyed American jobs. Between 1976 and 2005, America imported more goods than it exported every year. Thirty years in a row of trade deficits! Over that time, America imported over five trillion dollars of goods more than it exported. Five trillion! Yet somehow the economy added over 50 million additional jobs during that period. From 1960 to 2005, America exported more food than it imported. Forty-six years of agricultural trade surpluses. If deficits create jobs, shouldn't surpluses create them? Yet between 1960 and 2005, agricultural employment fell from 5.5 million to 2.1 million. During that time, while agricultural employment was falling, total employment in the overall economy doubled! Surely, deficits and surpluses are irrelevant for employment."

"I guess it's hard to argue that trade deficits hurt employment, Dave."

"Even if you worry about trade deficits, most of the obvious ways to get rid of them are very bad for a country. A recession would 'improve' America's trade balance because it lowers demand for foreign products. A bad investment climate would lower foreign investment in the United States, and that would push America's trade deficit toward zero. And then there's banning imports, which gives you balanced trade: balanced trade at close to zero. If you don't import anything, as we discussed before, it is very hard to export. The net result is higher prices, less innovation, and Americans trying to make everything for themselves. The most important thing to remember about trade balances, positive or negative, is that they are the result of economic factors and not the cause. The next time America has a recession and America's trade balance 'improves,' pundits will say that the 'improvement' in America's trade balance is the silver lining to the recession. But it is nothing of the sort. It is the flip side of the recession, nothing more and nothing less. But there is one ironic side to the trade deficit debate."

"What's that, Dave?"

"Remember when I told you that some of the critics of free trade made fun of me for being old-fashioned and out-of-date?"

"Yes. They said you didn't anticipate the modern economy. Mobile capital and all that."

"Here's the irony. Worries about the trade deficit go back to the fourteenth century! The 'economists' of the day believed that the wealth of nations depended on exports exceeding imports in order to acquire gold. Mr. Smith disabused the world of the notion that gold is the source of a nation's wealth. And trade deficits do not reduce a nation's wealth. It's not the age of a theory that matters. Just the logic."

"So I shouldn't be too worried about trade deficits. And when Americans import more than they export, it doesn't necessarily mean that American products are being treated unfairly."

"That's right, Ed. But it also doesn't mean that American products have the same access to foreign markets as foreigners have to America."

"So maybe it's not fair after all. Isn't fair trade just as important as free trade? Shouldn't the American government do something to level the playing field?"

CHAPTER

12

Fair Trade versus Free Trade

"I suppose you could make a case for government intervention on the basis of fairness if you thought the government could actually do something positive. 'Fair trade' or 'leveling the playing field' are usually code words announcing an attack on the consumer. Take charges of dumping, for instance."

"What's dumping?"

"Dumping is selling below cost."

"Why would a manufacturer sell below cost?"

"Because they make up the difference on volume. Sorry. That was a tired joke even 150 years ago. A good question: Why would a seller sell at a loss? One answer would be to penetrate the American market, weaken or destroy American competitors, and use that leverage to exploit American consumers by raising prices."

"But that doesn't make sense, Dave. After the seller penetrates the American market, it will have to increase the price well above the original level to make up for its earlier losses. This will alienate consumers. American producers, even if they couldn't afford to match the price cuts of the earlier period, would now find it profitable to reenter the market. With prices back at their original level, the dumper won't be able to recoup its earlier losses. The strategy looks disastrous."

"Bravo, Ed, bravo! But here is an alternative argument. Suppose a Japanese company lowers its price below cost and the American firms in the industry match the price cuts. If the Japanese firm is patient, it can drive the American firm out of business. If it is very costly to shut down a plant and reopen it, then the American firm may choose to shut down for good rather than be part of a cycle of leaving and entering."

"But they don't have to shut down, Dave. All they have to do is refuse to match the initial price cuts of the Japanese."

"But who will buy from them if they have higher prices, Ed?"

"It depends. If no one buys from the American firm, then the Japanese find themselves serving the entire American market at a price at which they are losing money. They not only have to absorb the production of the American companies, they have to make even more than this because they have stimulated demand with their lower price. This would surely be a back-breaker. To avoid these enormous losses, the Japanese company would have to limit the number they are willing to sell at the low price. This allows the American firm to still make sales and profits at its old price."

"Again I applaud you, Ed. Unfortunately your logic failed to convince everyone. Ultimately it came down to an empirical question. Did foreign companies who were accused of dumping eventually succeed in raising prices?"

"Well?"

"A number of industries came to be dominated by foreign companies because of their low prices. American firms went out of business or turned to other products. But the prices stayed low, even when American competition disappeared. All kinds of consumer products that were made overseas such as watches, calculators, and cameras became inexpensive and stayed that way. The televisions we saw at Circuit City are a perfect example. Asian firms accused of dumping electronic goods seemed to leave prices perpetually at a level that was allegedly below cost."

"But that's impossible!"

"Correct. Maybe the foreign companies were running their businesses like charities, selling products to the American consumer below cost. Seems unlikely, so maybe they weren't dumping in the first place."

"But if they weren't dumping, what was going on?"

"Can't you see?"

"They must have had a cost advantage of some sort."

"Exactly."

"I can think of two kinds of cost advantages, Dave. One is that they were better than we were at making televisions or some other product. But the second advantage would be an unfair one. Maybe their government was subsidizing their production."

"This was a common claim, advanced by the American producers who were trying to compete. But their argument was mostly irrelevant. Let's take the extreme case where the Japanese government subsidizes televisions or cars so heavily that the Japanese give them away to the American people. Can you think of a greater boon for a nation than to have a foreign nation using its scarce capital and labor to produce your goods for you without charging for them? That would be a wonderful world for America."

"But, Dave, if the Japanese government gives the Japanese producers a subsidy and drives the American producers into bankruptcy, we're at their mercy. We have already closed down our car or television factories, and the Japanese can jack up the prices."

"That argument sounds a lot like one you just rejected."

"I rejected the argument that a foreign company would incur enormous short-run losses and recoup those losses by charging much higher prices in the future, while hoping that American firms wouldn't reenter the market. But in the case of a government subsidy, the government absorbs the losses. The Japanese firm doesn't have to worry about the losses when considering cutting prices."

"Let's look at the issue from the other side of the Pacific. Rice in Japan can cost more than five times the price in the United States because of Japanese restrictions of foreign imports. Suppose Japan were to allow U.S. rice into Japan and suppose, for argument's sake, American farmers can supply all of Japan's rice needs at such a low price that Japanese farmers do not find it profitable to grow rice. What do you think would happen?"

"Japan would eventually pave over its rice fields, and the United States would have a monopoly. They could raise the price and take advantage of Japan. How could Japan start up those fields again? They couldn't—it would be too costly. Even if they did try to start from scratch, how would they know the United States wouldn't drop prices again and make them lose a lot of money? If I were a Japanese rice lover, I'd be plenty scared."

"Tell me, Ed. Where do you buy the wood for the cabinets of your televisions?"

"A lumber supply company outside of Chicago."

"Do you ever worry that they would double the price they charged you or even increase it 25 percent overnight?"

"No."

"Why not?"

"The guy knows I'd take my business elsewhere."

"How do you know that a new supplier won't try to charge the same inflated price your old supplier wanted to charge?"

"I'd just say no and call someone else. Besides, the new guy would want my business. If anything, he'd give me a price cut to start using him."

"Don't you think that the same force of competition among suppliers would prevent American rice growers from exploiting the Japanese once the Japanese became 'dependent' on U.S. rice? There are lots of rice farmers in the United States who would be competing for Japanese customers. But even if the U.S. government took over the rice market and tried to run it as a giant monopoly to exploit Japan, the Japanese could still turn to suppliers in other countries. So unless rice grows only in a handful of places, the Japanese would have nothing to worry about."

"Then why does Japan keep out American rice?"

"Why would American television manufacturers try to keep out Japanese televisions? Oh, they would certainly talk about protecting the American consumer from inferior foreign products, but that would not be the real story, now would it?"

"OK, OK. I see the point. You're saying that American firms went out of business because Japan could produce the goods more cheaply. Competition among Japanese firms and those from other countries kept prices low. Both Japan and the United States were made better off. And dumping is unlikely to be a profitable strategy."

"Right. Unfortunately, in the America with imports we visited earlier, the U.S. Department of Commerce did not define dumping as selling below cost. The Department of Commerce ruled that a foreign producer was dumping anytime that producer's price in the United States was below the price in its home market. The implication was that it was selling below cost in the United States."

"It could be true, couldn't it, Dave?"

"It's conceivable, but unlikely for reasons we discussed before. Prices can differ in two markets for innocent reasons: because of short-run currency fluctuations or differing market conditions. Measured price differences do not imply a predatory motive. The Department of Commerce was uninterested in such issues, however. Acting at the behest of U.S. companies trying to handicap foreign competitors, the Department of Commerce simply compared the two prices."

"Seems straightforward."

"It was not. The Department of Commerce took the average price in the foreigner's home market over the preceding six months. As long as any of the transactions in America took place below that average, even if the average U.S. price was above the average foreign price, the foreign producer was declared guilty of dumping. Normal market fluctuations in the price of the good or the exchange rate could then easily lead to a judgment of dumping. The Department of Commerce made numerous other arbitrary decisions in measuring quality and other aspects of the good. Politics pushed them toward a finding of dumping when none was actually there."

"Can you prove they were biased, Dave?"

"Between 1986 and 1992, for example, the Department of Commerce ruled on 251 cases of alleged dumping. They found evidence of dumping in 97 percent of the cases."

"That does seem rather high. What happened after the Department of Commerce found the foreign producer guilty?"

"The U.S. International Trade Commission, or ITC, then determined whether U.S. competitors were harmed by the low prices. The ITC found such harm in 68 percent of the cases where the Department of Commerce found dumping."

"What happened to the producer found guilty of dumping?"

"An antidumping fine was then imposed for each unit sold. The amount of the fine was equal to the difference between the 'fair' price, as calculated by the Department of Commerce, and the price in America."

"So it's like a tariff."

"Very much so. For example, if the 'fair' price was judged to be $8, and the item sold for $6 in the United States, the foreign producer would have to pay $2 for every unit sold in the United States. It acted like a 33 percent tariff. The average fine at the end of the 1980s was over 50 percent of the United States price. You can see how an antidumping order encouraged foreigners to raise their prices to avoid the fines. The consumer was harmed in the name of 'fairness.' Between 1985 and 1989, over 50 different products were hit with antidumping fees or countervailing duties, a similar fine. The average American citizen at the time would conclude that dumping was a common economic phenomenon, when in fact, it may never have actually occurred."

"But some of those cases could have been actual dumping, Dave."

"Highly unlikely. Here's my favorite example. It's not atypical, particularly for goods that came from Communist countries. Poland was once accused of dumping electric golf carts into the United States market. There were no sales of golf carts in Poland. Hard to believe there was dumping going on, but the Department of Commerce had to make a ruling. What did they do? There was no price in Poland to use as the 'fair' price. In such cases, the Department of Commerce finds a nation whose economy is similar to Poland's. They chose Canada. They compared the price of Canadian-made golf carts sold in Canada to the price of Polish-made golf carts sold in the United States."

"You mean they didn't use the price that the Polish manufacturer charged in Canada?"

"No. They used the price a Canadian manufacturer charged there and assumed it equaled what the Polish firm would have charged in Poland."

"Seems a bit of a stretch."

"Agreed. But lo and behold, dumping was discovered using this creative definition. A few years later, the decision was reopened. This time, the government didn't use Canada."

"Why not?"

"Who knows? Could it be because if you used Canada there would be no violation? Instead, the Department of Commerce took a different approach, which is allowed by the law, called 'constructed value.' It involved constructing an estimate of cost, then adding on 8 percent for profit to get what the price would be in the foreigner's home market."

"How did they estimate the cost?"

"As you can imagine, there is a wide range of estimates you can come up with, depending on how you deal with overhead and numerous other issues. The 8 percent is purely arbitrary and rather changes the concept of selling below cost. For products from Communist countries, it was even more creative. Because Poland was a Communist country, wages and other prices were set artificially, instead of by the market. Using Polish wage rates might lead to low estimated costs, a low estimated Polish price, and no finding of dumping. So the Department of Commerce used Spanish wage rates."

"Spanish! Why Spanish?"

"I know it's hard to believe, but again, it's purely arbitrary. A foreign producer would like to avoid being charged with dumping, filling out a 100-page questionnaire in English, and then being hit with a potentially massive fine. But a wary producer would have no idea in advance which country would be chosen to determine whether dumping was taking place. You can imagine what such a process did to the foreign supplier's incentive to compete on price."

"But there must have been some cases where the Department of Commerce found a foreign supplier guilty of dumping and the price really was less than cost."

"It's possible. And if true, consumers would benefit. But suppose you really wanted to stop such behavior. Do you see why a law against dumping, even a well-intentioned one, is so likely to backfire? Implementing such a law is in the hands of the politicians. Instead of fairness, you get a world where the Department of Commerce uses arbitrary procedures and finds dumping 97 percent of the time. Ultimately, the consumer is the loser even when the government is stopping genuine dumping. By the way, there was another insidious effect of the American antidumping law."

"What was that, Dave?"

"Turnabout was fair play. Other nations countered American law with antidumping statutes of their own, modeled on the U.S. law. For example, Monsanto sold Nutrasweet, a low-calorie sweetener, in Europe and the United States. Nutrasweet was protected by a patent, but the patent ran out in Europe before it ran out in the United States. Monsanto faced competition in Europe. Guess where the price of Nutrasweet was lower?"

"Europe. Monsanto had competitors there."

"Correct. But because the price in Europe was lower than in the United States, Europeans imposed a 75 percent antidumping fee, or tariff, on Nutrasweet sold in Europe, even though Monsanto was selling well above cost in both markets. Monsanto built a Nutrasweet factory in Europe, not because it made economic sense, but just to avoid the 75 percent fee. The European producers of Nutrasweet substitutes got rich at the expense of European consumers, and the world got poorer as less trade occurred."

"OK, Dave, I see how laws against dumping are a pretty costly way to 'level the playing field.' Is there another way to level the playing field while encouraging more trade?"

"A favorite is to threaten foreign nations with some form of retaliation if they do not lower their trade barriers."

"Does it work?"

"I cannot think of a single example. Barriers are not there because of some persuasive economic theory arguing they are good for the nation. They are in place to enrich domestic producers. Remember the case of

Japanese rice? The Japanese political system gives a disproportionate weight to votes from rural areas. So Japanese rice producers have an inordinate amount of power. Will the threat of tariffs on Japanese automobiles encourage the Japanese government to allow rice imports from America? The threat does not reduce the political power of Japanese rice producers in the Japanese parliament. Ask yourself, Ed, how Americans would feel if the Japanese threatened America in a similar fashion."

"But if the threat of imposing tariffs and quotas doesn't work, what should a nation do to reduce trade barriers outside its borders?"

"You do the best that you can for your own citizens and open your markets to products from all over the world. If Japan won't let in American rice or even American cars, as it is alleged, then ignore them. Allow their cars into America free of tariff and in any number. Give the American consumer cheap cars. America will become wealthy, and the rest of the world will notice. This is precisely the policy my nation, Britain, followed with great success in the nineteenth century."

"But why not use the threat of imposing a tariff to get foreign nations to reduce their tariffs?"

"Perhaps, if the threat is effective. After some point, a threat that is never carried out is no longer credible. If you want to maintain credibility, eventually you have to carry out the threat and impose tariffs in the name of opening the markets of your trading partners."

"Is that so bad?"

"Yes, if it fails to affect foreign trade barriers and only ends up hurting American consumers. Moreover, I find it hard to take the motivation seriously. The possibility that a tariff will encourage foreigners to reduce their barriers allows the protectionist politicians to have their cake and eat it too. Take a Congressional representative whose home district is in Michigan or Missouri where a lot of auto plants are located. Such members of Congress are invariably protectionists, trying to raise the wages of a small but vocal subset of workers in their districts."

"That's their job, isn't it?"

"I can't say. By helping one group of constituents, the representative harms the larger, but more diffused, interests of those constituents who buy cars and who work in other industries. This would bother me less if these politicians were more candid. But call them protectionists and you will be greeted with a look of shock and horror. 'Me, a protectionist? You wrong me, sir. I favor free trade. But I also favor fair trade. Let the other nations of the world practice free trade, and we will join them. In fact, we'll encourage them to take the path of free trade. We'll punish them with tariffs until they get rid of their own. Not to enrich the special interests of the manufacturer and the automobile worker who contribute to my campaign and who vote for me. Oh, no. Patriotism is my motivation. And to encourage the rest of the nations to see the light.' Thus is self-interest cloaked in patriotism and altruism for propaganda purposes. There is no evidence that such schemes are effective in lowering the barriers of other nations. They mainly keep wages in Missouri and Michigan higher than they would be otherwise."

"It does sound like 'Alice in Wonderland' to call yourself a free-trader while always voting for tariffs."

"Such members of Congress have other excuses to salvage their public image. They will tell you that free trade works fine 'in theory.' Or that free trade works only if the rest of the world follows free trade. These are rhetorical arguments to cover the smell of narrow self-interest."

"Is there any truth to the idea that free trade only works if everyone follows it?"

"Why should there be? Why should the benefits from free trade to America require an assumption that all nations follow free trade? Let me make it very simple. Suppose European farmers use their political power to keep out American farm products. America can accept or refuse European products. Which is better for America? Unless the refusal of European products causes them to change their policy, all you are doing is harming your citizens because the European governments see fit to harm their own."

"So the best strategy is to unilaterally promote free trade?"

"Yes. Although the United States, for much of the last half of the twentieth century, took a multilateral approach and tried to get the nations of the world to lower their tariff barriers en masse."

"You must have approved of that."

"In principal, yes. It's a nice idea to move the world toward freer trade. But ultimately, I think it would have been better for the United States to simply say that its borders were open and invite the nations of the world to trade."

"But wouldn't it have been better to get other nations to join us?"

"Yes, and sometimes they did. But the devil was in the details. A lot of these so-called free trade agreements might better have been called managed trade agreements. They were full of appendices and side agreements and codicils and addenda giving this or that product special treatment. This product wouldn't come in freely, it would still have a special tariff rate. That product would maintain its quota protections. Every one of these agreements became a political free-for-all. Because there was a possibility for special treatment, every industry would try to have its protections maintained. And even when an industry would lose its protection, there would be a phase-in period where the tariffs and quotas would often persist."

"That seems fair, Dave. That way the people in the industry would have a chance to make other plans and prepare for the challenges of having to survive in a free market without protection from competitors."

"True. But it also meant that the politicians could change their minds. Nothing political is writ in stone. The other problem is that when you have all those special exceptions and phase-ins, you inevitably have to create a bureaucracy to monitor compliance on both sides of the border. As this bureaucracy grows, its employees become less interested in free trade and more interested in fine-tuning this or that aspect of the next round of trade talks. But perhaps even worse than these effects were the educational consequences of these multilateral agreements."

"Educational consequences?"

"When an American president would make the case for free trade, he would inevitably become a mercantilist. He would—"

"A mercan*what*?"

"Sorry. A mercantilist is one of those folks we've talked about who believes that a nation's economic health depends on running a trade surplus. A mercantilist thinks imports are bad—they destroy jobs. Exports are good—they create jobs. They fail to understand that trade affects the kind of jobs a nation has rather than the number of jobs. They fail to understand you can't control exports independently of imports. They don't understand that a trade deficit is the flip side of a capital surplus."

"So what's that have to do with education?"

"Whenever a so-called free trade agreement was being considered, whoever was president of the United States would try to create support for the agreement among the public. He would talk about how great it was because it would open up foreign markets for American products."

"Nothing wrong with that."

"No, there's nothing wrong with American companies being able to sell their products to others. But that is not the point of trade. That argument made people think that America had to open its borders as the cost—the cost!—of getting other countries to open up their borders to American products. What trade is really about is getting the peoples of the world the chance to *cooperate* with each other, sharing each others' skills and doing what is wisest for each person and in turn, each nation. When the president made mercantilist arguments, it made people think that trade was a zero-sum game, where in order to get the benefits, you had to give up something. America would have benefited from opening its borders without 'getting anything' in return. When other nations opened their borders, the main beneficiary wasn't the United States but the people in those nations who now had access to American goods and services."

"So how did those multilateral approaches actually turn out?"

"The General Agreement on Tariffs and Trade, or GATT, began just after World War II. Overall, GATT was a success. Trade barriers fell, and world trade increased many-fold during the time of these agreements. There were problems, though. Nations committed to free trade could still follow protectionism by imposing antidumping fines as we've been discussing. And nations found other creative ways to try to circumvent the agreement. So the nations of the world set up a mechanism for adjudicating disputes and a forum for negotiations that would expand free trade further. They chose an unfortunate name, the World Trade Organization, or WTO. Putting 'World' in the title allowed opponents of free trade to demonize the WTO as some kind of sinister world government that threatened the sovereignty of nations."

"Did it?"

"If you sign an agreement to follow free trade and you expect the other nations of the world to do the same, you do give up some of your rights to keep out foreign products unless you want to back out of the agreement. But the WTO had no police or enforcement capability. The real problem with the WTO was that it canonized the multilateral approach and the bureaucracy for negotiating and monitoring trade. Rather than championing free trade, America championed negotiation and multilateral agreements. But most of the critics of the WTO had a different complaint. Let me tell you a story. Toward the end of the twentieth century, Americans became increasingly concerned with the environment."

"The environment?"

"It was related to what you would call conservation—a concern for clean air, water, and the preservation of nature and wildlife."

"Sounds good."

"It was. America passed something called the Clean Air Act to make sure that companies didn't emit too many unhealthy chemicals into the air. One aspect of the act was the 'cleanliness' of the gasoline sold in the United States. Some types of gasoline produce more chemicals than others. When the regulations were revised in 1990, foreign refineries had tougher standards to meet than American ones, no doubt the result of lobbying by American companies to keep out foreign competitors."

"What happened?"

"After the WTO was established, the foreign competitors complained to the WTO, claiming it violated the WTO because American companies were held to a looser standard. The foreign competitors were right. And they won their case at the WTO."

"What did winning mean? Could the WTO change American law?"

"No. Remember, the WTO had no enforcement mechanism. When America lost the case at the WTO, they had two choices. First, they could ignore the ruling. This would allow the foreign nations who had been discriminated against to put tariffs on American exports and still be in compliance with GATT. Rather a bizarre and ineffective punishment of America. Instead, such a policy punishes the victim. Second, the United States could rewrite its environmental regulations to give foreign suppliers the same rules as America's. America chose to give foreign suppliers the same regulations."

"Seems reasonable. Why was the WTO so controversial?"

"Some felt that the United States should have the right to discriminate against foreign products when writing environmental regulations. Why should the WTO have any say at all about America's environmental regulations? While that seems reasonable, it meant that domestic producers could use environmental regulations as a way to keep out foreign competitors. If you want cleaner air, it would seem much better to hold both American and foreign suppliers to the same high standard, rather than trying to go easy on American firms while being tough on foreigners. But in fact, every free trade agreement at the end of the twentieth century and the beginning of the twenty-first was controversial."

"I can understand that."

"I can, too. Change can be scary. What was interesting was that the critics of trade would play both sides of the fence."

"Meaning?"

"They said that trade was bad for the United States. And it was bad for the poor nations, too."

CHAPTER

Is Globalization Good
for the Poor?

13

"I worry about trade hurting America. Why would trade hurt poor people outside of America?"

"The critics claimed that the global trading system was rigged against the poor countries. They claimed that the so-called international organizations, organizations like the World Bank and the International Monetary Fund—the IMF—were bad for poor people."

"Were they?"

"Both organizations, but especially the World Bank, had the opposite mission, to help poor people around the world."

"How'd they do?"

"People who worked at the IMF said the IMF did a good job, but the World Bank was awful. People who worked at the World Bank said the World Bank did a good job, but the IMF was awful."

"Was either side right?"

"Unfortunately, I think they were both right. Neither institution did a very good job, though not always for the reasons given by the critics. The bottom line is that the greatest successes where people climbed out of poverty had little or nothing to do with the World Bank or the IMF. The greatest successes were those nations such as China and India—and Japan a generation earlier—that used trade, foreign investment, and more open domestic markets to improve the lives of their people. China's standard of living quadrupled—quadrupled!—between 1980 and 2000 as China opened its borders to foreign investment, trade, and private enterprise. India's standard of living doubled over the same time period. Those are remarkable achievements that lifted hundreds of millions of people out of desperate poverty. Nations that embraced free trade and foreign investment prospered. Nations that cut themselves off from the rest of the world suffered. The nations helped by the World Bank and the IMF typically stayed poor."

"Did the World Bank and the IMF have enough money to get the job done?"

"Alas, some might say they had more than enough."

"What does that mean?"

"The failure of the World Bank and the IMF to have any significant effect on poverty proves a profound point—how much you spend is often not as important as how you spend it. Between 1950 and 2005, the rich nations spent and lent hundreds of billions of dollars trying to help the poor. If intentions were results, world poverty should have been eliminated or at least dented. But intentions are not results. The money had little or no impact."

"But, Dave. You must be exaggerating. Hundreds of billions of dollars should have done something."

"Yes, they did something. They just didn't help poor people around the world very much. The money given or lent by the World Bank and the IMF was particularly ineffective."

"But why? Surely all that money should have made some difference."

"Much of it never got to the people it was intended to reach—the poor. A lot of the poor nations were ruled by rich thugs who became even richer by diverting international funds into their own pockets."

"They stole it?"

"Sometimes it was as simple as that. Sometimes they used the money to hire friends who were incompetent. Sometimes they simply failed to do what they promised with the money and squandered it. It is hard to monitor compliance in a dictatorship. But sometimes the aid failed because it was focused on a particular project, constructing a dam or an electric power plant or a factory that wasn't as productive as the planners had hoped. The irony, or maybe the right word is the tragedy, is that the World Bank and the IMF were seen as bastions of free trade. When these organizations failed to achieve their goals, they damaged the reputation of free trade and free markets."

"Were the World Bank and the IMF in favor of free trade?"

"Sort of. They said they were. But free trade and free markets are about allowing individuals to make their own choices. The World Bank and the IMF focused on telling governments what to do—build this dam or spend this money on education or build this government factory. Not surprisingly, a lot of those projects didn't turn out as well as was hoped."

"But surely it would help the poor living in nations without enough schools to build schools."

"You'd think so, wouldn't you? What could be more straightforward? One reason people are poor is that they don't have enough education. So build nice schools and nice classrooms with nice books and even, sometimes, computers."

"So were the schools never built? Did corruption keep the money from being used for education?

"Sometimes. But often, the schools were built. But the students didn't come. Their parents couldn't afford for their children to go to school. They needed them in the fields. Or the jobs that required a good education didn't exist in those countries. So there was no incentive to stay in school or to study. Bureaucrats with the best of intentions often don't have sufficient information to fully understand the full effects of what they'll actually achieve."

"So why did people consider the World Bank or the IMF free trade organizations?"

"The World Bank and the IMF didn't just fund dams and power plants and spending on specific goals such as education. Sometimes they'd encourage countries to lower their tariffs and to open their capital markets. Or they'd bail out a government of a fiscal crisis on condition that it get its financial house in order. They'd demand that the government receiving the funds balance its budget or reduce inflation or improve the performance of some state enterprise. Those changes didn't have much to do with free trade."

"Did those reforms work?"

"The conditions were often ignored. The whole idea of an international organization in Washington, D.C., with little accountability and limited information about the countries they were trying to help, micromanaging a macroeconomy, isn't much of a free market solution. Then there was the question of compliance. The World Bank or the IMF would demand a particular reform, but how could they verify whether the reform had actually been put in place? And if they decided that the nation receiving funds had failed to comply, they often found it hard to follow through with the threats of withholding the money. They would give the money anyway after a new promise by the leaders to do better this time. Incredibly, this would happen year after year, decade after decade."

"Why? Couldn't they just say no?"

"What often was needed was what is now called 'tough love'—withholding money and goodies when there's misbehavior. But bureaucracies don't make very good parents, tough or otherwise. Too much self-interest and not enough love. Water is thinner than blood. After all, the World Bank and the IMF were lending and spending agencies. That's what they did. They lent money to poor nations. They spent money on poor nations. They weren't as interested in collecting on the loans or spending the money wisely when they gave it away. There were no incentives for them to do so other than good will. And they were giving money to leaders who often had no incentive to spend it wisely. Is there any reason to think that it would turn out well?"

"You make it sound like nothing ever worked. Are you sure you're not exaggerating?"

"I wish I were. Yes, sometimes, in a few cases, there was real economic growth that was the result of a World Bank project or an IMF loan. But the record of failure was extensive and enduring, unfortunately. Here's an example. Between 1980 and 1994, there were 12 poor countries that averaged at least one World Bank or IMF loan per year. Those loans were conditional on the nations improving their policies. The median growth rate in those 12 countries was zero. Zero! Something's wrong there. Bizarrely, one of the criticisms of the IMF and the World Bank was that they were too demanding or too market oriented. The critics wanted the World Bank and the IMF to give away more money or forgive the loans that had been made in the past. But the biggest problem wasn't the demands of the World Bank or the IMF. It wasn't their so-called market orientation. It was the corrupt and inept governments they inevitably ended up accommodating despite the best of intentions. The critics of these organizations usually blamed the United States for their failure."

"But didn't you say that the World Bank and the IMF were *international* organizations?"

"I did. And they were. But they were headquartered in the United States. A lot of their funds came from the United States. People claimed that the World Bank and the IMF were pawns of multinational corporate interests, whose real mission was to keep people poor or to enhance the power and influence of the United States. The critics claimed that the whole world trading system was designed to enrich the United States at the expense of the poor people of the world."

"That's a pretty depressing thought if it's true."

"Corporations like to make money. That's why they exist. And they will certainly try to bend institutions to that goal if they can. Their control over the World Bank and the IMF and the world trading structure was exaggerated. The real problem with the claim that the World Bank and the IMF were pawns in some grand scheme of the United States is that the World Bank and the IMF had no real power. The nations that accepted their aid and their conditions—whether they followed those conditions or ignored them—did so freely. The critics noted the same poor performance that I've explained to you and blamed the World Bank or the IMF or the United States. But the real blame belonged with the governments and the leaders of the poor nations who kept taking the World Bank aid or the IMF loans. Why did they keep taking the money? Why did they keep taking the loans? It was those governments and those leaders who failed the poor people of those countries, not the World Bank or the IMF or the United States or multinational corporations. That having been said, there were certainly cases where powerful special interests twisted the rules of trade in their own favor."

"For example?"

"In 2005, the United States signed a trade agreement call CAFTA, the Central American Free Trade Agreement. It was to create free trade between Honduras, El Salvador, Costa Rica, Panama, Guatemala, and the Dominican Republic. But as I mentioned before when we talked about so-called free trade agreements, it was full of exceptions and phase-ins and special provisions for particular industries. One of the most bizarre provisions was to limit imports of sugar into the United States from the Central American countries."

"I guess that is bizarre. A free trade agreement that limited imports."

"It was stranger than that. While the agreement didn't allow free trade in sugar, it did allow an expansion of imports, a giant increase equal to 1 percent of U.S. sugar consumption."

"Did you say 1 percent?"

"Yes. The word 'giant' was just a little sarcastic. Yet, the sugar industry in the United States became the main opponent of the agreement. Even that 1 percent was too much for them to swallow. To reduce the political cost of voting for the agreement, other provisions were added that made trade under the agreement less free. When it finally passed, maybe they should have called it CAMTA, for the Central American Managed Trade Agreement. But as strange as that was, think how strange it was to the Dominican Republic and the other countries in the agreement, where desperately poor people were eager to work growing and harvesting sugar to sell to rich Americans. Yet America was essentially saying to them that they wouldn't be allowed to get the benefits from free trade because of the political power of a handful of sugar beet and sugar cane farmers in a handful of states. And of course, the American consumers paid as well for that enrichment—the price of sugar was about double what it would have been under true free trade. That made all kinds of food and drink more expensive in America than they otherwise would have been. That was the kind of policy that America championed that hurt the case for true free trade and opened up America to the charge that it was hurting the world's poor. But there were other claims about America and the world's poor that made no sense."

"Such as?"

"People liked to point out that America was 5 percent of the world's population yet enjoyed 25 percent of the world's income. Those who saw this as an injustice viewed the world as a zero-sum game—if America was rich, America's wealth must have come from somewhere. Obviously, said the critics, it had come from the poor nations of the world. After all, they were poor, weren't they? But America wasn't wealthy because the other nations were poor."

"But didn't you say that America got wealthier because they were able to buy inexpensive products from China and Mexico and Indonesia?"

"Yes, that benefited consumers in America. They had more money to enjoy other products they couldn't have afforded otherwise. And the workers and employers and stockholders in those industries making those products—they benefited, too. But people in Mexico and Indonesia and China also benefited. Millions of people in those poor countries improved their standard of living. Not high by American standards. But higher than before. Do you think the Chinese or the Indians or the Mexicans would be richer if they had refused to trade with America? Those people were poor, yes. But not as poor as they would have been if they hadn't been part of the global economy. Here's another way to see it. Suppose Americans suddenly decided to work half as hard and spend more time reading and hanging out with their families, and so on."

"America would be a lot poorer."

"In monetary terms, yes. Americans would presumably be richer in other, nonmonetary ways. Presumably, they'd enjoy spending more time with their family more than the goods and services they could have enjoyed by working harder. That would be the reason for their decision to work less and enjoy more leisure. But Americans would have less income. Americans would no longer enjoy 25 percent of the world's income. But that income and those resources wouldn't be magically freed up to go to poorer citizens of other nations. The goods and services that Americans had created when they worked harder simply wouldn't exist. The rest of the world would have a higher proportion of world income. But that's only because the denominator would have decreased. If anything, because there would be fewer trading opportunities with the United States, the rest of the world would be poorer. The lost income in the United States wouldn't be available to the poor people in the world now that Americans weren't getting it. But there is one way Americans being wealthy does make the rest of the world poorer."

"How's that, Dave?"

"Americans like to enjoy the money they earn. They work hard and take that money and enjoy all the goods and services that result. They could, instead, give it away. They could give it to the poor around the world. If Americans kept less, others could have more."

"That sounds like simple arithmetic."

"It seems that way. But most Americans don't want to work hard in order to send the money overseas. They work hard to improve their own lives and the lives of their families. So claiming the rest of the world is poor because Americans like to enjoy what they've made seems a bit strange. But I think Americans would give more of their hard-earned money to poor people outside of America if they thought it would make a genuine difference. And there were always experts urging the governments of the rich nations of the world to be more generous. Yet, those efforts had never worked in the past. All that foreign aid had a trivial impact on poverty. The law of unintended consequences trumped the good intentions of the donors."

"But that sounds like an excuse for doing nothing. When you say that foreign aid has been a failure, are you saying that nothing can be done, that nothing *should* be done?"

"I'm saying that when you find yourself in a hole, stop digging. You certainly shouldn't dig faster or get a more expensive shovel."

"So what should be done?"

"The rich nations of the world should open their borders to the products and the skills of the poor people of the world. The rich nations should stop subsidizing a handful of their own wealthy farmers. That punishes American taxpayers and the poor around the world, whose best use of their skills is often farming but who cannot compete with subsidized American and European crops. The rich nations should stop trying to create good economies in countries with bad governments. It doesn't work. The rich nations of the world should stop sending money to corrupt autocratic governments with leaders who keep the money for themselves. That creates an incentive for those leaders to keep their poor people poor. If the rich nations are to give away money, they should give money *after* reforms are made rather than as a condition for reforms that are never made. The rich nations should give money to nations that open up their economies and reduce the number of poor rather than rewarding nations that keep their poor people poor. Those are all political policies. Rich individuals in rich nations should encourage their governments along those lines. But as individuals, they should give charity to organizations that help creative and ambitious people in poor countries get the capital they need to create economic prosperity, what is called microlending. And finally, the rich nations and the rich citizens of those nations should stay away from well-intentioned policies that not only leave the poor no better off but actually make them worse off."

"For example?"

"The critics of free trade wanted workers in poor countries to have the same labor standards as American workers. The same minimum wages, the same safety standards, the same overtime provisions, the same standards for clean air and clean water as America."

"Those sound like good ideas."

"Maybe. Some of the loudest advocates of labor standards were American unions. They said they cared about poor people but I suspect that self-interest was a large part of their motivation. By the end of the twentieth century, the proportion of the private U.S. workforce that was unionized was below 10 percent. Open borders and open trade meant that a lot of foreign workers were doing jobs that used to be the backbone of the union movement in the past. Requiring foreign countries to have stricter environmental regulations and higher safety standards and higher wages would have helped American workers at the expense of the poorest workers around the world. So I suspect the labor leaders in America were less than altruistic."

"But why would you care about their motivation, if the result is better working conditions for poor workers?"

"The real question is whether poor workers would be better off."

"Are you kidding, Dave? How could workers be worse off with higher wages, safer working conditions, and cleaner air?"

"The tragedy of Mexico and Kenya and other poor nations is that their people have little education and few skills. If we tell American corporations that they have to pay American wages and benefits to Mexicans and Kenyans, those corporations won't have much of an incentive to open factories in the poor nations of the world. I don't think it does the poor people outside the United States any good to keep out low-wage foreign employers if the alternative is even lower wages paid by their own domestic companies. If you want, I could talk to the people Upstairs and arrange for us to go back to the America of 1850. Wages and work conditions in America were appalling in those days. If America had adopted the labor standards of today in the America of 1850, it would have crippled America's growth. America today might look more like the America of 1850."

"But what about the air and water, Dave? Shouldn't American factories operating overseas or in Mexico abide by American standards for clean air and water? Wouldn't the Mexican workers want to live and work in places with clean air and water?"

"Perhaps. It depends on the consequences. You have to ask yourself why a nation like Mexico didn't adopt the same standards as America to start with, and whether the problem is best entangled in trade issues or addressed separately as a domestic problem for Mexico to deal with."

"Why didn't Mexico adopt the same standards for clean air and water?"

"Such standards are expensive. America at the end of the twentieth century in a world of trade was the wealthiest nation in the world. America could afford cleaner air and water. But people in the poorest nations struggled to survive. For America to demand that every nation have the same elevated standards for air and water quality takes remarkable arrogance. It would be like requiring citizens in every nation to have cars as luxurious as those driven by Americans, to eat sirloin steak every night, to have houses and yards as big as those in America. It would be like—"

"I think I get the idea, Dave. But clean air and water seem pretty important."

"They are, especially when you're wealthy. But if all the nations of the world had the same clean air and water standards as America, kids would starve to death because the jobs available to their parents would pay considerably less. That's important, too. You know, Ed, maybe we should go back to the 1800s. We could look at industrial London with its dark skies of soot and smoke, or we could visit the Mississippi River."

"Why the Mississippi, Dave?"

"We'd see a river filled with pollution—all kinds of debris and waste. People in the 1800s would have preferred a cleaner river, but it was too expensive. Because they tolerated a dirty river then, America was able to eventually get wealthier and sustain an unparalleled standard of living alongside clean air and water. If Americans want Mexico to get cleaner air and water without starving her people, they might show the same patience America needed to get cleaner air and water. Let Mexico grow economically, get wealthier, and then the people of Mexico will choose cleaner air and water on their own. That's the way it happened in the United States and the way it happened in other nations that were successful economically."

"But what if that dirty Mexican air drifted over into Texas, Arizona, or California? Then wouldn't Americans have a right to complain about those Mexican factories?"

"Certainly they would. The question then becomes, what is the best way for Americans to get the Mexicans to clean up their air? If Americans want Mexicans to have cleaner air, either out of altruism or selfishness, should Americans pay for it or should the Mexican people? Should such concerns become part of a trade bill, or should they be addressed in a separate agreement that focuses on the environment? When Americans demanded that Mexicans clean up their air as part of a trade bill, they were holding back Mexican growth. They made Mexicans pay for clean air by lowering their standard of living."

"But was it fair to American workers that their factories had higher standards than the Mexican ones? Isn't that an unlevel playing field again?"

"Sure it is. And it's one of a million differences between doing business in Mexico or Indonesia and doing business in the United States. I wonder if Mexican workers thought it fair that Americans were better educated, had more computers and equipment to work with, and benefited from every other advantage that accrued to American workers. The goal of trade policy is to give people the opportunity to live their lives in interesting and rewarding ways, not to make sure that everyone has exactly the same opportunities. If American workers thought it was such a great advantage to have lower standards in Mexico, they could go live there. In fact, all the foot traffic ran the other way."

"So the bottom line is that free trade is good for America as well as for the nations and the people America trades with?"

"Yes. One of the contributions of my theory of comparative advantage was to show that even poor nations benefit from trade. The road to wealth for a nation is quite simple. Use your resources wisely. By resources, I don't just mean the traditional natural resources of fertile land, oil, and minerals, but the know-how, education, ingenuity, and drive of the people. Using your resources wisely means giving the people the incentive to work hard, to innovate, and to take risks. And opening your markets to trade to allow your people to leverage the skills of people in other nations. All rich nations where even the poorest people are relatively affluent have the rule of law, secure private property, relatively open borders to trade, and relatively free markets internally."

"You make it sound simple, Dave."

"It is simple. But establishing the rule of law and securing private property is not so simple. And there are nuances of culture and government that help unleash the power of economic freedom. If those aspects are missing, prosperity won't necessarily follow. Economists still have much to learn about the role that culture and government play in making markets work well in poor countries. But nations that are open to the world do better than nations that are not. If we want to help poor people around the world, we need more open governments and more open trade."

CHAPTER

CHAPTER

14

Self-Sufficiency Is the Road to Poverty

E d looked lost in thought, which I took to be as good a sign as I might hope for. Finally he looked up with a puzzled expression. "Dave, can you explain to me again why everyone is driving Ford Fairlanes and Chevy Impalas?"

"This is the world where Frank Bates becomes president in 1960 and gets a bill passed so that America allows no imports. You are looking at an America after 45 years of self-sufficiency. Let me remind you of the sequence of events. It started with the quota on Japanese imports of televisions. When people saw how your workers prospered, they wanted protection for their industries. Usually such efforts fail. I have been given the power to let you see what would happen if such efforts succeeded and all foreign products were banned."

"Dave, I understand the power of free trade now. What I don't understand is why a world of no trade is so bad. After all, self-sufficiency is a virtue. It's better to be self-sufficient than to depend on others."

"It would appear that way. But self-sufficiency is the road to poverty. You told me you don't grow your own corn. But you could at least imagine it. How about making your own shirt? How long would it take you to grow your own cotton, spin it into thread, and weave your own cloth? You would be self-sufficient. Wouldn't it be better to depend on the cotton farmer, the thread spinner, and the cloth weaver? Is it not clear that to make your own shirts and shoes and grow your own food is to lead a life of bitter poverty?"

"OK, but you're taking a good idea to a ridiculous extreme. Just because it's hard to be completely self-sufficient doesn't mean it's a bad idea to be a little self-sufficient."

"I agree, Ed. It usually is good to be a little self-sufficient. It is also good to 'depend' on others. Neither is a virtue in its own right as long as you define your terms correctly. When you buy shirts from a department store, you're dependent on a long chain of people beginning with the farmer in Egypt, perhaps, who grew the cotton, down to the owner of the department store. But is there anything negative about this dependency? You and the others in the chain benefit from your purchase of the shirt. It surely is superior to growing your own cotton and doing all the other steps yourself."

"I understand that in the case of an individual, but why should it apply to nations? What's it have to do with all these Ford Fairlanes everyone is driving?"

"Remember when you got that bill passed banning imports of Japanese televisions?"

"I guess that was an extreme version of a quota."

"Right. Remember how all your workers got rich?"

"Sure. I realize now that some of that wealth was illusory."

"Not to them. Their wealth was real. Those were real cars they were able to buy and real vacations they were able to take. They did not know of the wealth lost to others. What was illusory was assuming that the gains your workers experienced were the total effect of the quota. The total impact on America was negative when you included the harm to television consumers and others."

"But, Dave, you told me before they were driving Corvettes and Cadillacs. How did those cars turn into Ford Fairlanes?"

"Other industries followed yours in asking for protection from foreign competition. What was good for television workers must be good for those in automobiles, textiles, and every product. President Bates proposed a bill forbidding all imports."

"Was there any opposition to the bill?"

"Oh sure. A bunch of economists took out an ad in the *New York Times* calling it a disaster. But people have always made fun of economists, calling them 'slippery,' 'charlatans,' and every other name in the book. Some economists deserve those insults. But economists are close to unanimous about free trade. People didn't listen. Congress passed the bill, and President Bates signed it. It was hailed as a landmark in American history. And it was."

"What happened then?"

"Not much, at first. But slowly, changes took place. Without imports to put dollars in the hands of foreigners, industries that relied on exports faltered or collapsed. Remember that movie your grandson was watching, *Toy Story*?"

"Sure. I liked it quite a bit myself."

"It never got made. Disney stopped making new films in the early 1980s."

"Why?"

"Exports were a significant share of their profits. Without those profits, Disney didn't have the incentive to hire enough cartoonists and designers to make new movies. They just show their old films now."

"That's a shame. I liked that movie."

"Disney was one of many companies that never grew to their full potential. Other companies never even came into existence. For example, Bill Gates is a car mechanic. He—"

"Who's Bill Gates?"

"Sorry. Bill Gates would have been a billionaire in a world of free trade. Without free trade, he leads a modest life tinkering with cars."

"Is it so bad if we lose a billionaire and gain a regular Joe making a modest living?"

"It probably doesn't thrill Bill Gates. But the real loss is America's. You only see one man's income being lower. The real loss is the industry he helped transform—computer software—and the products that he brought to market. Those products made him rich. But they also enriched the lives of millions of others. He started a company called Microsoft. Its products would have been used all over America and the world if there were free trade."

"But, Dave, he could still sell the product in America, couldn't he? Aren't there enough Americans who can buy innovative products?"

"There are many Americans to buy his products. But without imports and the roundabout way of production, America cannot have everything it enjoyed with free trade. To make Microsoft a great company, Bill Gates needed the skills of countless programmers, marketers, and distributors of his product. There are a limited number of those people to go around. Motorola, Boeing, Disney, Apple, and Google were all competing for those talented people."

"Why were there plenty of them in a world of free trade and not enough in a world of self-sufficiency? Isn't the population the same in both cases?"

"The population is the same. But the jobs being done by the working-age members of that population are not."

"If Motorola and those other companies have high-paying jobs, why won't the talented people end up there under self-sufficiency?"

"When America stopped allowing imports, certain vital products were no longer available from overseas."

"For example?"

"Oil. Textiles. Shoes. Cars. Steel. Consumers turned to the American producers of these goods."

"That must have been good for those American producers."

"You might think so, the same way your workers and your company flourished when Americans were forced to buy your televisions instead of having Japanese televisions to choose from. But when every industry is in the same boat, you don't get the same effect."

"Why not? And why was the overall effect on the economy so negative?"

"Think of it as the roundabout way to wealth wreaking vengeance. When your industry prospered because of trade restrictions, we talked before about how consumers suffered more than television companies gained. Why was that?"

"Televisions got more expensive."

"Right. Consumers had to pay more for televisions. But there were other effects, as well. When the television industry expanded, it drew workers, capital, and raw materials away from other industries. America lost the goods that those industries would have produced using those resources. A single industry can expand and enrich itself at the expense of other industries and consumers, but not all industries can expand simultaneously. There are not enough workers, capital, or raw materials to allow it."

"I understand the principle, Dave. I just don't see why it has to be that way. You say there are not enough workers to go around. But all the workers who were employed making goods for export will now be available to produce the imports."

"That's right, but there was a reason to produce the goods the roundabout way rather than the direct way. America gets poorer producing everything the direct way. When the television industry benefited at the expense of others, the harm to the country as a whole was spread thin so it was effectively hidden. When every industry pursues protection, the impoverishment of the country is out in the open."

"I don't see why it has to happen, Dave."

"Think about all the goods America used to import that will now have to be produced domestically. Take all the steel and all the cars and all the watches and all the calculators and all the wool and all the cotton and all the sugar and all the coffee, all the toys and all the clothes and all the rest. Stack them to the sky. How was America able to enjoy all of those goods under free trade?"

"The roundabout way?"

"The roundabout way. Under free trade, all over America, workers and machines make goods the roundabout way—by making things Brazilians want and trading them for coffee and shoes, by selling pharmaceuticals and airplanes to Japan and trading them for cars and calculators and video players. Use your mind's eye to put those workers and machines all in one place. In one giant industrial park are all the chemists and the aerospace engineers and marketers and distribution people and the factories and offices they work in. They are the real resources America uses to get imported goods. Imagine them all gathered together."

"I see them."

"When America stops importing, all of those people are going to have to make the watches and the shoes and all of the other products America used to import. They will have to produce the nearly 2,000,000 motor vehicles that come from Japan, even after Japanese companies build factories in the United States. They are going to have to grow the cotton and the coffee and bring the oil out of the ground that used to come from abroad."

"OK."

"Go to the gate of this enormous industrial park. Tell the order clerk: 'I want 2,000,000 cars, and so many pounds of sugar and coffee, this many computers and this many watches . . .' and so on; a year's worth of the goods that America imports. You tell the clerk you will be back in one year to pick up the goods. The clerk takes the order into the park. Do you think they will be able to fill the order?"

"Of course not. You can't expect chemists from Merck to be able to find oil or Boeing assemblers to be able to make cars in an airplane factory."

"True. Let's give them a chance. A miracle takes place. The machines from the airplane factory become an automobile assembly line. Take all the existing factories and turn them into factories for the things they need to make now."

"It's still impossible. The workers don't have the right skills."

"Let there be another miracle. Those Merck chemists who now have to be in the oil business? Let them instantly have degrees in petroleum engineering with all of the knowledge they would have acquired in school. Let all the workers have the knowledge they would have acquired if they knew all along they were going to be in the watch business or the television business. Do you think they could fill the order?"

"I don't know. I would think so."

"They can't. It can't be done. The head of the park will find that no matter how the workers are mobilized with their newfound skills, the order can't be filled. The head of the park will have to bring new workers into the industrial park, build more factories there, or bring in more machines to be used in new factories. The park will be booming, but it will be booming just to match the production of watches, cars, and so on, that America used to import. Meanwhile, outside the park there are fewer workers and machines available to produce everything else. So the total amount of goods America can enjoy must go down."

"How do you know that the workers inside the park can't fill the order without bringing in extra people and resources? Why won't there be enough land, factories, and machines?"

"The roundabout way to wealth. Suppose Boeing sells 25 planes per year in Japan, and it takes 10,000 workers and a certain amount of raw materials for Boeing to make those planes. Suppose the revenue from those planes allows Americans to buy 200,000 cars from Japan. But it will take more than 10,000 workers and raw materials to make those 200,000 cars using the direct way, instead of the roundabout way."

"How do you know?"

"If it took fewer than 10,000 workers, then Boeing, or someone else, could produce the 200,000 cars using fewer resources. They'd have lower costs. They could earn more profit making cars instead of planes. It is not because Americans are less skilled than the Japanese at making cars;

they're just a lot better at making planes, and that is a more efficient way to make cars."

"But American cars are just as good and just as cheap as foreign cars. Why can't American cars replace foreign cars as cheaply and efficiently?"

"American cars are just as cheap and just as good as foreign cars. But this equality is misleading. Your wife Martha bakes her own bread now and then, doesn't she?"

"You bet, and it's better than you can buy in the store."

"If it's better than you can buy in the store, she must bake often. Does she ever buy bread in the store?"

"Sure, Dave. Baking bread takes a lot of time. It's not worth it to make it all the time. She bakes when she finds the time."

"So she imports bread into your household to go along with domestic production."

"You could call it that."

"Don't you see the paradox, Ed? If your wife's bread is better than she can buy in the store, isn't it irrational to buy some at the store? You just told me hers is better."

"It is. It's just that some days she's tired or busy."

"It may make sense to bake some of your own bread. But that doesn't imply that baking *all* the bread you eat is a good idea, even though the occasional home-baked loaf is better and cheaper than a store-bought loaf."

"Why not?"

"Think about how Martha and you would feel if the government banned the sale of bread and you were not allowed to 'import' bread into the economy called your household. Martha might shrug and say, 'It doesn't matter. My bread is just as good as store-bought, it's cheaper, and I even enjoy baking bread.' But suppose that to bake all of the family's bread, Martha must make multiple batches. She would find that the additional loaves she bakes would be much more expensive than the ones she used to buy. The money expended on the additional loaves is still less than the cost of store-bought bread. But the money is only part of the cost. If Martha bakes all of her household's bread, it's going to take a lot more time than when she baked occasionally. The cost of that extra time is much higher, too."

"How can that be?"

"Because the true cost of the time spent baking is not monetary. It's the lost activities Martha no longer enjoys because she is busy baking."

"You know what else, Dave? She probably wouldn't replace the lost store-bought bread loaf-for-loaf with her own homemade loaves."

"Why not, Ed?"

"When she bought the bread in the store, the cost was the same for each additional loaf. But you are right; each homemade loaf gets more and more expensive as she has to give up additional activities in or outside of the house to do more baking. At first, she gives up relatively unimportant activities. As her time spent baking bread expands, the things she stops doing get more and more valuable. So we might choose not to eat as much bread as we used to. We'll be worse off because we'll have less bread and fewer shared activities."

"Bravo, Ed. I salute you. It is the same principle we discussed before when we talked about how in the face of a quota, domestic production will not expand enough to make up for lost imports."

"I see it now."

"And I hope you also see how the equality of price and quality of American goods and foreign-made goods does not imply that America can replace foreign imports without a cost."

"But why is the nation like a household? Why do cars get harder to make?"

"Imagine America having to start up enough new car factories with new workers to make the 2,000,000 cars that used to be imported. To do so would mean drawing productive capacity and workers away from other industries. America would no longer enjoy what those workers used to make. In addition, the workers in those factories producing an additional 2,000,000 cars couldn't be as productive as the workers making the first 2,000,000 cars made in America."

"Why not? Wouldn't they adopt the same technology?"

"They would, presumably. But the workers and managers would not execute the technology as artfully, efficiently, and cheaply as the people already doing it. The first 2,000,000 cars are made by those Americans with the strongest interest and skills to work in an automotive factory. The managers in those factories will be the best at motivating and leading those workers to productivity. As you open more factories with more workers and managers, you no longer get the best ones. You start attracting workers and managers who are less efficient than the ones initially attracted to the industry. It gets more and more expensive to make a car. Eventually, in the case of cars for America, it becomes cheaper to make cars the roundabout way via imports rather than to produce more cars by opening car factories."

"I don't know, Dave. It seems like making a car is just making a car. Can't anyone figure out the steps on the assembly line?"

"Doesn't everybody know how to throw a baseball in America?"

"Sure."

"Do you think the worst ten pitchers in professional baseball are just as good as the top ten?"

"No."

"It's the same way with working in an auto factory or running one. Some people are better than others—some are better at taking direction.

Others are better at leading and managing. Take your television plant in Star. Did you just hire people at random because anyone can figure out how to assemble televisions? Were all your plant managers equally good at motivating workers?"

"No, but it's still not easy to understand."

"Think of it this way. In a world where imports are allowed, Japanese and American cars of similar quality sell for a similar price. This leads to the conclusion that American cars are just as good as Japanese cars. But this is only true at the current levels of production where America, because of imports, does not have to make all of its own cars domestically. Eliminating imported cars will increase the price of domestic cars. A decrease in supply leads to an increase in price. Another way to see it is that an increase in the demand for American cars cannot be satisfied without a price increase. And now you should understand why. Ford and GM and Chrysler can't afford to make up for the lost imports without a higher price because of the higher costs of building larger and newer plants."

"I see that, Dave."

"But that is only part of the story. The other fallacy in assuming that America does not need foreign supply is to believe that innovation will continue. Without imports, the Ford Fairlane would not have become the Taurus, and without foreign cars to prod American car manufacturers today, American cars will never become whatever they can become in the next 40 years."

"It's still hard to understand how all the effects of no imports lead to such an overall loss in standard of living. I'm struggling to see all of the connections."

"Think of Martha baking all of that bread, or even some of it. Think about what life would be like if you had to make everything yourself. Your house would have less of everything because Martha's and your time is limited. If you are forced to make everything for yourself, your command over goods and services has to fall. America's house looks the same way when there are no imports."

"It's still kind of hard to see everything that's going on, Dave."

"Here is another way to see it. In international conflict, a nation will try to place an embargo on its enemy. Why? To impoverish the enemy. How? By cutting off its ability to interact with the rest of the world. Putting up tariffs and quotas, or in the extreme, deciding to be self-sufficient, is to place an embargo on oneself. Does that sound like a beneficial policy?"

"I guess not. But if I were alive in 2005, I think I'd still feel guilty if I were one of those Americans buying a car from the Japanese."

"Then you have learned nothing tonight. If you buy an American car, you are helping the American autoworker and the stockholder in American car companies. If you buy a Japanese car, you are helping the workers of

Merck and Boeing and their stockholders and executives. And in a world of open trade, the whole idea of a 'Japanese' car or an 'American' car is just an attempt to deceive buyers into thinking they are doing something patriotic when they buy 'American.' As we discussed earlier, a lot of Japanese brands are built in the United States. A lot of American brands are built outside of the United States. Both kinds of cars use parts from all over the world. But even if every so-called American car was made by Americans using all American parts and every foreign car was made outside the United States using foreign parts, you should still buy the car you get the most value from. The American auto manufacturer asks you to buy American so that America is not dependent on foreigners. But it is easy to keep Americans from buying foreign cars—make a higher quality product at a lower price. The American manufacturer who can't succeed in the marketplace asks the government to keep out the Japanese cars or impose a 'voluntary' quota. The reduction in supply drives up the price of American cars, as we talked about before. That increase in price is really a welfare payment. It's a hand-out imposed on the car buyer to help out the auto manufacturer. Talk about a failure to be self-sufficient."

"Take it easy, Dave, you're getting excited."

"In my condition, Ed, a heart attack is not a big worry. Why should guilt enter into a consumer's decision? If the Stellar Television Company made an inferior or overpriced television, would you expect people to keep buying your product because they felt sorry for you? Is that the road to genuine self-sufficiency? True self-sufficiency is not demanded of others as an arbitrary rule, but earned. What do you think happens to productivity when a worker or firm knows that no matter how shoddy or poorly pro-duced the product is, people will buy it out of guilt or pity? People should buy the products that give them the best value for the money."

"But, Dave, if America became so poor because imports are banned, why didn't people get rid of the laws that keep out foreign goods? Couldn't people see they were getting poorer?"

"Sure, but people were scared. They didn't blame protectionism for their poverty. When economists proposed reopening America to the world, people worried about their jobs. What would replace the jobs they already had, if foreigners were allowed to compete? How would you vote if you were an engineer in the American oil industry in Louisiana, a watchmaker in Massachusetts, or a worker in a textile mill in the Carolinas? Getting rid of quotas would cost you your job."

"But you argue that other jobs will arise to replace them."

"People couldn't see that. Not only did they fear the transition between the old world and the new, they couldn't imagine the computer chip, portable computer, or pharmaceuticals yet to be discovered to fight disease. There were no industries like that even to imagine. People were content to hold on to what they had."

CHAPTER
15
The Choice

"Dave, you've worn me out. Can I see how my kids turn out in an America without trade?"

"Of course. I do get a bit long-winded at times. It's the politician in me. Remember that your children's lives are going to be very different from how they were with free trade. When we saw them before, Steven was running a computer software company, and Susan was running a business on the Internet. Their lives are going to be different when there is no free trade."

"Why?"

"Because the world we are in now is the world where America is self-sufficient. The opportunities available to your children will not be the same."

"So how is Susan doing, Dave?"

"She's doing fine. She has three children, two girls and a boy. She is married to a fine man. They live in Star."

I took Ed to Susan's house. Susan never made it to graduate school or to Hong Kong. She spent her time raising her family. We watched as Susan put the kids to bed and finished cleaning up the kitchen.

"She looks pretty happy to me, Dave."

"I daresay she is. Far be it from me to argue that doing without foreign products makes you unhappy. Just poorer than you might otherwise be."

"There's nothing wrong with raising a family."

"Certainly not, Ed. The question is whether Susan should have the opportunity to choose a different life. In a world without imports, the choices she faces are more limited."

"How about Steven?"

"He's here in town, too. He's running the Stellar Television Company."

Steven lived in a nice house on a quiet street off Main Street. We watched Steven helping his son Justin with his math homework. There was no big-screen television or voice-controlled computer. Just a math book, a pad of yellow paper, and a dining room table.

"Why are Justin's glasses so thick, Dave?"

"Remember when we visited Justin before, his father wouldn't let him watch the movie for too long? He still can't watch much television because it's too tough on his eyes. In the world of free trade, he controlled his eye problem with a drug Merck developed. They weren't able to develop that drug in a world without trade, so Justin wears glasses instead. The glasses work almost as well."

I didn't tell Ed, but the people Upstairs had given him a break. Without that Merck drug, Justin would have lost his eyesight entirely. But the people Upstairs thought that if Ed's grandson went blind under a world of no imports, Ed's choice about whether to support Frank Bates wouldn't be an exercise of free will. It's easy to love free trade if it can keep your grandson from going blind.

"Steven seems pretty happy too, Dave."

"He does seem to be. I can't allow you to talk to Steven. If you could, you could ask him what it is like working for the same company his father did, and his father before him."

"It was good enough for me."

"I know. But whether it is good enough for him is a more complicated issue. Think back to a boy in 1960 with his dreams. Now you only see the man."

"The man seems happy. Sure, Star isn't as lively as it was under free trade, and we don't have juice bars, Circuit City, or iPods. But I like Star the way it always was."

"I doubt it. You like the Star of 1960, but I doubt you'd like the Star of 100 years earlier when there was horse manure in the streets, children had rickets, and women died in childbirth with much greater frequency. You like what you are used to. But I'll accept part of what you say. Money and wealth are not everything. Nor is America with free trade a paradise. Free trade leads to more opportunity, more wealth, and a more dynamic world. But a more dynamic world does not benefit everyone."

"And what will happen to the people who are not creative, who can't go to college, and who don't dream of changing the world? What will they do, Dave?"

"There are still jobs for people without a college degree. There are just fewer jobs in manufacturing than there once were. When Federal Express—a company that delivers packages overnight—creates 225,000 jobs in the United States, they're not all for MBAs. They have jobs across the entire spectrum of skills. Retailers on the Internet still have warehouses with people driving forklifts. But free trade hurts some people. So does protectionism. You saw what America looks like when there is self-sufficiency and America keeps all the jobs."

"But maybe Frank Bates made a mistake. Maybe he shouldn't have banned the import of all goods, just the import of high-wage goods. He should have allowed Americans to import coffee, cotton, and crude oil, but kept the high-technology, high-skill, and high-wage jobs in America."

"Ed. Don't look at the jobs. Look at the people. If Americans are good at flipping hamburgers because they have low skills, then they will end up flipping hamburgers. You can't turn a hamburger flipper into a computer software designer by banning imports of computer software and 'saving' those jobs for the hamburger flippers to take. Well, you can. But it will end up making America poorer, not richer. You can help a low-skill individual through protectionism by punishing other Americans with high prices. Is that fair?"

"I don't know."

"Ask yourself if it is wise. If a group of Americans do not compete well in the global marketplace because their skills are readily available around the globe, how should America respond? By protecting them and insulating them from the competition they face, or by encouraging them and their children to improve their skills? I hope you have learned tonight that the choice America faces is not between more jobs or fewer jobs. The real choice is between a dynamic world and a static world—a world of encouraging people to dream and acquire the skills to make those dreams come true and a world of encouraging people to be content with what they have and to dream less."

"Which is better, Dave?"

"That is for you to decide. I will leave you with one thought. In the Bible, in the Book of Deuteronomy, God addresses the Israelites and tells them: 'I have set before you life and death, a blessing and a curse. Choose life.' Many biblical commentators have asked why God implores or commands the Israelites to choose life. What kind of a choice is there between life and death? It's no choice. It's obvious you should choose life. So why does God demand the obvious? Perhaps God was not referring to a literal choice between life and death but a spiritual choice between experiencing life versus fearing life's experiences and running away from them. Choose life, Ed."

"But which life, Dave? They both look inviting, I—Hey! Dave! Dave! Dave!"

I was gone. My time was up and Ed was on his own, back in his den in 1960 in Star, Illinois. Frank Sinatra was still pouring his heart out on the hi-fi. Martha slept in the next room. Steven and Susan were children, sleeping the sleep of children, down the hall. Down the road, the Stellar Television Company was locked up for the night, awaiting another day of production. Televisions were the only product in America where foreign competition was completely banned. Epcot Center and Disney World were a gleam in Walt's eye. There were no personal computers. No VCRs. No *Toy Story*. No Federal Express. No Google. They hung in the balance of time, unrealized.

Ed sat stunned for quite some time, staring at the piece of chocolate cake and the glass of milk that still sat on the table in the den, as fresh as when we left them, worlds ago. Ed finally drifted off to sleep. . . .

"Honey, wake up! You've got to make that speech for Frank Bates in Los Angeles. You'll miss your plane."

"Martha!"

"Ed, why did you sleep out here? I'll help you pack. You better jump in the shower."

Ed didn't say much. Martha wasn't surprised. She knew Ed had a lot on his mind. She just didn't know how much.

Ed made his plane to Los Angeles for the convention. He took his speech with him, the same one Frank Bates had sent him, nominating Frank for president. As I looked on from Upstairs, my heart sank, but I did not despair. I knew there was still time.

On July 14, 1960, at 11:00 A.M. on a breezy Los Angeles day, a taxi pulled up to the front doors of the Beverly Hills Hotel, and Ed Johnson stepped out. He checked in, headed to his room, and told the hotel operator to hold all calls and wake him at 4:00 P.M. He slept soundly. A good or a bad sign, I did not know.

Ed rose, showered, and put on a clean shirt and a suit. He took a taxi to Santa Monica and the beach. He walked along the beach for an hour, then found a bench in a grassy park, looking out over the water that separates the great economies of Asia from the United States. He sat there for a while, watching the Earth spin forward and bring the sun down into the ocean. Then he caught a taxi to the Sports Arena where the convention was being held. He still had his speech with him. I was not encouraged.

Time passed slowly for both Ed and me. The crowd was an undulating mass of banners, buttons, and placards. The Frank Bates supporters had their share of signs: Put America First; Free Trade is Unfair Trade; Protect American Jobs—Keep Out Foreign Products. And my favorite: If Americans Buy Foreign Products, Where Will Our Children Work? Finally, Ed's turn came. He was to make a key nominating speech for Frank Bates. The journalists and television cameras were ready. Now Ed was ready, and he began to speak.

He read from the speech he had brought, the one Frank Bates's staff put together. He spoke of Frank Bates and the success of the Stellar Television Company. He spoke of Star, his hometown, and what makes Star special. It was really what makes every small town in America special. The open hearts of its people. The simplicity. The constancy of life. It's a good life, and Ed described it well. You could feel the pride of the people listening. Many were from Chicago, Los Angeles, and New York City, but their pride in small-town America was real.

"In my hometown of Star, the rough edges of life are smoothed by the familiar. You know your neighbors because you've lived next door to them for years. Your friends are friends for life, and your family is there to share good times and bad. My father was born in Star, founded Stellar Television Company, and died there. I was born in Star and will live there till I die. My children were born there, and they, too, will likely die there."

At that line, Ed hesitated and looked lost for a moment. I could hear him repeat the line to himself, "My children were born there, and they, too, will likely die there." I wondered if he was seeing Susan in Hong Kong, or Steven, running his own company out in California.

Ed took a deep breath. I took one too. There wasn't much time left. When Ed started to speak again, he put his speech aside and looked straight out at the crowd.

"I don't often come to Los Angeles. I'm always a little bit uneasy before I arrive. It's noisier and faster. It's different from Star, and change is always threatening. But after a few days, I usually feel at home in Los Angeles, Chicago, or New York. Not enough to want to stay, but enough to understand why so many of you choose to live here. Noisier and faster, yes, but something else as well. There's more life here.

"Of course, we have our share of excitement down in Star. A new film comes to the Bijou every month. Even in Star, and in all the small towns across America, we have our dreamers and achievers, our people who yearn to remake the world. In Star, it might be a young boy who dreams of running his own factory. In another town and place, a boy hears the lonely whistle of a train and dreams of writing a great novel.

"America would not be America without the big and small cities. I recently took a trip to a foreign country."

Ed paused. His eyes roamed through the great arena waiting for the words to come that would unlock what waited in his heart.

"When you go away from home, you miss the familiar patterns that make up the life you know. Breakfast with your wife. Taking a walk with your kids after dinner and showing them the stars. The hometown paper, your barber, and the greetings of the people when you arrive at work. These are little things. But in America these little moments have a richness and vitality missing elsewhere.

"Do you know why? Because America is still the land where everything is possible. In America, when a parent talks to a child, they may speak of the present, but the future hovers over them like a promise.

"Coming home to the America I love, I am reminded of America's greatness and uniqueness. It is the vitality of America that makes her great. Some of that vitality comes from our people. But much of that vitality comes from the laws and institutions of America that set us free to come alive and make the future keep its promises. We must safeguard the flame that is at America's core, the flame of creativity, of change, of life. God bless you, and God bless Frank Bates. Good night!"

The crowd roared its approval, but I wasn't sure what or whom they were applauding. Probably a little of Ed Johnson, a little of Frank Bates, and a lot of America. When the crowd finally settled down, people tried to understand how Ed's speech fit in with Frank's protectionism. Some found a link between protectionism and protecting the American way of life. But others said Ed had never mentioned protectionism and maybe had denied its virtues. They couldn't understand why he'd thrown away the end of his speech to speak about America's greatness. They said he betrayed Frank Bates.

I thought he had. I might have wished for a more direct statement about the evils of tariffs and quotas, but sometimes the roundabout way is best. . . .

CHAPTER

A Final Word from David Ricardo

16

Did Ed Johnson betray Frank Bates? A tough call. A young fellow out of Massachusetts got the nomination that year and went on to the White House. Frank Bates ran for Congress again the next time around and lost narrowly. Did Ed Johnson destroy Frank's career? I think not, though Ed's speech didn't help Frank. It was a tightrope act from a man trying to keep the respect of a politician and his respect for himself. Most people couldn't understand the speech and chalked it up to political naiveté. They blamed Frank Bates for letting a businessman address the convention and toss away the end of a speech Frank Bates's boys had written.

Some people blamed Ed anyway. Frank did. He never spoke to him again, which was probably fine with Ed. Ed retired from the television business. He sold his company to the Japanese on the promise that they keep the plant in operation for at least three years to give his workers a chance to look elsewhere.

Some people called Ed names behind his back and to his face. Ed took the worst of it with a smile. He lost some friends. Some people never understood and didn't want to understand; even Ed might have had difficulty explaining himself. Finally he stopped trying and contented himself with his wife, his hobbies, and taking trips to Boston and California to see his grandchildren.

As for me, perhaps my story holds as much interest for you as Ed Johnson's. I wish I could tell you the details, but I've signed a variety of pledges promising to keep the details private. You know how they are Upstairs. Free will and all that. I can tell you that things have turned out a bit brighter than I thought possible. What's it like? I'm afraid I can't say. I can tell you that Ed's speech has gotten me over some hurdles, but there are more still to come. The afterlife is like life that way. Just when you think you've reached the top, another set of peaks loom on the horizon. They ask more of some; less of others. So it goes.

I am allowed to tell you one spot of information. The key for my defense was that point about choosing life. Not the way you might think, getting in good with the Boss by quoting one of his favorite books. It doesn't work that way Upstairs, you know. No, the key was getting away from the economics, narrowly defined by standard of living. Don't misunderstand—I had the economics on my side. But money isn't everything. I'll tell you a secret that my pledges don't cover: Economists understand better than anyone that it's not really about money but about striving and living and dreaming.

If my story has given you any pleasure, I would ask one favor of you. Since my time as an economist, it has become fashionable to mock my profession for our alleged indecisiveness and the splits in our ranks over various questions. I may have done a poor job explaining the ideas of comparative advantage to the students of the world. But I have had much success with the economists. Even those who make theoretical arguments against free trade are loath to advocate tariffs and quotas in practice. So at the next cocktail party when someone tells a joke about the one-armed economist being unemployed because he can't say 'on the other hand,' or how if you laid all the economists end to end, they still wouldn't reach a conclusion, don't encourage them with the false laughter such dull-wittedness provokes. Smile a knowing smile and tell them that you have heard otherwise on the question of international trade, and from a very old but reliable source.

To all those who lie awake at night thinking of what might be—sweet dreams.

CHAPTER

Explanations, Sources, and Additional Reading

STAR, ILLINOIS

There is no town of Star in Illinois. The Stellar Television Company never existed. However, between 1948 and 1974, Motorola ran a television factory in Quincy, Illinois, producing Quasar televisions. They sold that plant to Matsushita in 1974 on the promise that they would keep the plant in Quincy. Matsushita closed the plant in 1976, citing poor conditions in the television industry. They kept in operation another plant purchased from Motorola in Franklin Park, Illinois.

The town of Quincy had about 42,000 people in 1960. At its peak, the Motorola factory employed about 3,000 workers and made about 2,000 televisions sets a day. In 2000, Quincy's population was 40,366.

I have used employee reminiscences and stories of the Motorola plant in Quincy as background and inspiration for Star and the Stellar Television Company. I am grateful to Doug Wilson and Judy Nelson, news editor and librarian, respectively, of the *Quincy Herald-Whig* for background information and sources. I am grateful to Lois Tyer, reference librarian at the Quincy Public Library, for reading me a story about the reunion of Motorola workers, five years after the plant closed. I thank Robert Meyer, former assistant superintendent of Quincy High School, for his memories of the effect that the plant closing had on the kids of Quincy.

I am grateful to the workers from the plant who spent time talking to me: Joy Viar, former line supervisor; Robert Morris, former foreman; Carl Swed, former plant manager; Lee Webster, former engineer; Steve Moody, who worked on the receiving dock; Donna Moody, former cafeteria worker; Jane Slater, whose jobs in the plant included wiring, soldering, and key operator; Joanne Felker, former bookkeeper; Oneta Burner, former cook and cashier in the cafeteria; and Chris Schork, who did a variety of tasks in accounting, inventory, and payroll.

These former workers still have a strong loyalty to Motorola and gratitude for the years they spent working in the plant. One of them told me that her husband would not take the road by the plant when she was in the car, because she would start to cry. They all felt Motorola was a fair and good employer. They spoke with fondness of the dances, skating parties, and the company picnic. None spoke bitterly about the sale of the

117

plant to the Japanese, though some resented the Japanese owners for closing the plant. Although all expressed varying degrees of sadness on the plant closing, the common assessment was that most workers did find work within a year of the closing.

The Broadcast Electronics Company opened a plant in Quincy about a year after the Motorola plant closed and employed some of the laid-off workers. I wish to thank Cathy Ellerbrock and Steve Wall of Broadcast Electronics for putting me in touch with former Motorola workers. Others found work in town at the Harris Allied Broadcast Company and MicroENERGY. Some of the workers found new work at a Ford seat belt factory across the river in Missouri, which closed after a few years.

Everyone I spoke to felt that the loss of the Motorola plant was a tough blow for Quincy, but everyone felt that their children, the next generation of Quincy, were better off than they were. As one put it, "They may sing the blues, but they have everything. Two cars. A house full of furniture. Some even have a boat." One former worker said that most of the college-educated kids don't find opportunities in Quincy and instead settle elsewhere. The most revealing comment I heard that relates to the arguments of this book was an assessment of the virtues of working at Motorola. "It was a stable family atmosphere. There was no point in getting extra education for a different job you might not like."

LIBERTIES

To dramatize the choice facing Ed Johnson and America, I have taken various liberties. America has changed a lot since 1960, and all of those changes are not due to the relatively open borders of the United States with the rest of the world. I doubt that restricted trade policies would have left small-town America unchanged, nor is the increased labor force participation of women, for example, due to the relatively open borders of the United States between 1960 and today. The explosion of women's labor force participation, however, does illustrate the flexibility of labor markets to respond to change. I apologize to the Democratic Party for what may be historical inaccuracy. In 1960, protectionist Frank Bates may have more likely been a Republican. Today, even though the Republican Party is more protectionist than it was 15 years ago when I wrote the first edition of this book, protectionism still finds a readier home in the Democratic Party, so I have made Frank Bates a Democrat.

It is important to remember that the real America of today is not a world of free trade. America has thousands of tariffs and quotas on a stupendously detailed array of products. While the average effective tariff rate on all imports is now below 2 percent, the International Trade Commission estimates in their most recent study (in 2004) that trade restrictions currently reduce U.S. well-being by $14 billion annually. I encourage the reader to visit the Web site of the International Trade Commission where you can find the tariff level on any product by visiting their tariff database (http://dataweb.usitc.gov/scripts/tariff2005.asp). Search a simple phrase such as "plates," and you will enter the Kafkaesque world of trade restrictions. In addition, as discussed in Chapter 12, antidumping laws allow tarifflike fees to be assessed without politicians having to vote for them. Such fees are depressingly numerous.

FACTS AND FIGURES

I placed Ed Johnson in 1960 because that was the beginning of the surge in Japanese television imports. I have tried to take data from 2005 where possible. Otherwise, I have tried to use the most recent data available. Some of the numbers used in this edition vary from earlier editions due to revisions in various government data series.

Chapter 3

The length of time a worker must toil to buy a television was calculated as follows. It is not easy to get retail prices for 1960. I used the 1960 Sears catalog. The cheapest 21-inch television that was able to receive both UHF and VHF sold for $180. Average weekly earnings in the manufacturing sector in 1960 were just under $90. This number is calculated from Table B-47 of the *Economic Report of the President*, 2005, which lists hourly wages in the manufacturing sector of $2.15 per hour and average weekly hours of 39.8. So the average manufacturing worker needed a little over two weeks of work to be able to buy a television. In 2004, the average manufacturing wage was $16.15 per hour or roughly $128 per day. The Circuit City Web site currently has a 20-inch color Jensen television for $93—less than a day's work. The price of the cheapest remote control model in 1960 was $380, about a month's salary for a manufacturing worker at the time. The modern television is a color television of superior quality measured by reception and particularly by maintenance and durability.

So even though America has become reliant on foreign-manufactured televisions, the relevant real price measured by how long it would take a manufacturing worker to earn one is dramatically lower. The figure would be very similar for workers outside of manufacturing.

Chapter 4

In Chapter 4, I discuss the improvement in the American standard of living between 1960 and today. When the American economy went through a recession in 1991, many people argued that the American economy had been stagnating since 1973 and blamed this on the Japanese. I argued in the first edition of this book that this was an impossible case to make on either theoretical or empirical grounds. This issue has become of smaller concern due to the economic growth in the 1990s, an awareness of the flaws in the CPI in capturing quality, and the death of the Japanese scapegoat as the Japanese economy has floundered. But given the history of that debate, I thought it useful to keep the facts in this edition. The figures presented on the relative standard of living between the United States and Japan are taken from the *OECD World Factbook*, 2005. The most recent data using purchasing power parity are from 2002 and show U.S. per capita GDP at $36,121 and Japanese per capita GDP at $26,954. The U.S. figure is 34 percent above the Japanese.

In 2003, the Bureau of Labor Statistics changed from an SIC classification to an NAICS classification and changed the historical data back to 1964. So hourly earnings in 1960 from earlier tables are not comparable to current data. So I used the 2002 number that is consistent with the previous 1960 data, then imputed wage growth based on the growth from 2002–2004 to get a figure for 2004 ($15.48) that is roughly comparable to the 1960 figure of $2.09. These hourly earnings figures were in turn deflated by the CPI-U-X1 consumer price index (Table B-62, *Economic Report of the President*, 2005) to get the increase in real terms discussed in the text of 26 percent.

The CPI overstates inflation and thereby understates increases in the real standard of living. The Bureau of Labor Statistics has an improved price index, the CPI-U-RS, that goes back to 1978. Using that series for inflation between 1978 and 2004 (also in Table B-62 of the *Economic Report of the President*, 2005) gives an increase in real hourly earnings between 1960 and 2004 of 34 percent, rather than the 26 percent figure used in the text. But even this price index overstates inflation because of the inability of the Bureau to correct for quality changes. For one example of this bias, see "Measuring Growth from Better and Better Goods, NBER Working Paper No. 10606," by Mark Bils of the University of Rochester.

To get a measure of worker compensation inclusive of fringe benefits, I have used Table B-49 from the *Economic Report of the President*, 2005, also from the Bureau of Labor Statistics. I have used hourly nominal compensation for the business sector, deflated by the CPI-U-X1. This shows an increase between 1960 and 2004 of 93 percent. Again, this inflation measure overestimates inflation, so this figure of 93 percent is understated. For per capita gross domestic product figures, I have used Table B-31 of the *Economic Report of the President*, 2005.

These numbers will surprise some readers. We hear constantly that the average American has seen no improvement in standard of living since the 1970s. I think these claims come from focusing on wages rather than compensation, ignoring the inability of the CPI to control for quality changes and ignoring changes in the composition of the workforce over the last 40 years as the labor force participation of women has grown dramatically. I hope to have more systematic evidence on this issue available on the Web in the near future.

Data on the labor force participation of women, the number of jobs in the United States, and the proportion of the workforce in agriculture are taken from the *Historical Statistics of the United States*, the *Statistical Abstract of the United States*, and the *Economic Report of the President*, 2005. I thank Harold Brown, Phyllis Otto, Michael Murphy, and Karen Kosanovich of the Bureau Labor Statistics for their help in tracking down various numbers.

The figures on employment and real wages in the information technology sector come from *Accelerating the Globalization of America: The Role for Information Technology*, Institute for International Economics (2006), by Catherine L. Mann and Jacob Funk Kirkegaard,

In 2004, the proportion of 18- and 19-year-olds in college reached an all-time high of 47.8 percent. This figure is taken from Table A-5b from the Current Population Survey and can be found on the Web at http://www.census.gov/population/socdemo/school/tableA-5b.xls

Chapter 5

Motorola employment figures are from the Motorola Web site.

The data on employment of women and women's labor force participation are from Tables B-36 and B-39 of the *Economic Report of the President*, 2005.

The decline in the proportion of the workforce in manufacturing from 28 percent in 1960 and 11 percent in 2005 is from Table B-46 of the *Economic Report of the President*, 2005. The 1960 numbers differ from the numbers in the earlier editions of this book due to the industry reclassification mentioned earlier, but the effect is the same—a dramatic decline in the importance of manufacturing as a source of employment over the last 40 years. The quadrupling of manufacturing output comes from Table B-51 of the *Economic Report of the President*, 2005. Measuring changes in manufacturing output inevitably involves making some heroic assumptions, but the bottom line is that America makes more stuff with fewer people than it did in the past.

The wage rate for manufacturing jobs relative to other sectors in 2004 is calculated from Table B-47 and Table B-46 of the *Economic Report of the President*, 2005. Table B-47 has hourly earnings for manufacturing and the private sector. Using the proportion of manufacturing employment in total private employment, I can adjust the private sector wage to compute a nonmanufacturing private sector wage rate. These calculations give a wage premium for manufacturing wages relative to nonmanufacturing wages of 3.5 percent in 2004. The *Economic Report of the President*, 2005, does not have data on nonmanufacturing wages going back to 1960, so I used Tables B-46 and B-47 from the 1999 report. As before, the 1960 numbers are not strictly comparable to the current numbers due to industry reclassification, but that does not affect the main point that manufacturing jobs pay more than jobs outside of manufacturing for the sample of workers surveyed by the Bureau of Labor Statistics.

Chapter 7

Estimates of the effect on American car prices caused by "voluntary" restraints on Japanese imports are taken from Robert Crandall's 1984 article in *The Brookings Review,* "Import Quotas and the Automobile Industry: The Costs of Protectionism."

Chapter 8

According to *Ward's Automotive Yearbook* of 1962, the Ford Fairlane and Chevrolet Impala were the two best-selling cars of 1960, so I have let them stay popular in the year 2005 in a world without imports. In the first two editions of this book, I contrasted these two cars with two of the best-selling cars of the mid- to late 1990s, the Honda Accord and the Ford Taurus. Honda is now number two behind the Toyota Camry. Ford discontinued selling the Taurus in America and replaced it with the Ford Five Hundred, not exactly an American icon, so I have left in the discussion of the competition between the Accord and the Taurus. The 1960 Ford Fairlane got 14 and 19 mpg in the city and on the highway, respectively. The figures for the 2000 Honda Accord were 23 and 30 mpg; the 2000 Ford Taurus got 20 and 28 mpg. The 2006 Accord gets 24 mpg in the city and 34 on the highway. These numbers are taken from the EPA Web site on fuel economy (http://www.fueleconomy.gov).

Chapter 9

In recent years, a number of economists have been making a theoretical argument against free trade. A formal exposition of these arguments can be found in Paul Krugman's *Rethinking International Trade*, MIT Press (1994). My take on these arguments is in Chapter 9.

Chapter 10

Background on the Concorde was taken from various articles in the popular press. Data on the Concorde's fares were found by calling British Air on September 6, 1999. A round trip on the Concorde, New York to London without advance reservations, was $10,297. British Air's regular fare without advance reservations for non-Concorde travel was $1,326.

The discussion of the impact of Sematech is based on "High-Tech R&D Subsidies: Estimating the Effects of Sematech" from the *Journal of International Economics* (1996) by Douglas Irwin and Peter Klenow.

Chapter 11

Figures for America's overall trade deficit and trade deficit with China are from the Bureau of the Census and can be found at http:// www. census .gov/foreign-trade/www/

Chapter 12

For additional bizarre details of the Polish golf cart case discussed in Chapter 12, see volume 57, *Federal Register* 10334 (March 25, 1992). Figures on dumping cases between 1986 and 1992 are from telephone conversations with Keith Anderson of the United States International Trade Commission. I also took statistics and information from Tracy Murray's and N. David Palmeter's articles in *Down in the Dumps: Administration of the Unfair Trade Laws*, edited by Richard Boltuck and Robert E. Litan. Further data on dumping cases and their distribution by country can be found in Keith Anderson's article "Antidumping Laws in the United States—Use and Welfare Consequences" in the *Journal of World Trade*, April 1993.

Chapter 13

This chapter draws heavily on William Easterly's superb book, *The Elusive Quest for Growth*, MIT Press (2002). A counterpoint can be found in Joseph Stiglitz's *Globalization and Its Discontents*, a strange book that finds no fault with the World Bank (where Stiglitz was chief economist) and instead blames the IMF for all bad things in the world. Jeffrey Sach's *The End of Poverty: Economic Possibilities for Our Time*, Penguin (2005), has a more optimistic view of top-down aid than presented in Chapter 13. Martin Wolf's *Why Globalization Works*, Yale University Press (2005), has much useful data and analysis on the impact of globalization on the poor around the world.

Chapter 15

The 1960 Democratic Party Convention was held at the Los Angeles Memorial Sports Arena from July 11 to July 15.

ADDITIONAL READING

I have tried to make any remarks about David Ricardo's economics as accurate as possible. His remarks on environmental issues, the WTO, and political issues are only my speculations. Ricardo's classic work is *On the Principles of Political Economy and Taxation*. It is not light reading. An online edition can be found at the Library of Economics and Liberty (http://www.econlib.org).

For an extraordinarily creative and lucid defense of free trade, read the essays of Frederic Bastiat. Start with *Economic Sophisms*, Foundation for Economic Education (1996), and then go on to *Selected Essays in Political Economy*, Foundation for Economic Education (1995). Bastiat died in 1850, but his work reads as if it were written a day ago to solve the problems of tomorrow. His work can be found online at the Library of Economics and Liberty.

A good textbook on international trade is *World Trade and Payments: An Introduction*, Addison Wesley (2001), by Richard Caves, Jeffrey Frankel, and Ronald Jones.

A good primer on trade, trade policy, and globalization is Don Boudreaux's *Globalization* (2007).

A delightful compendium of the ugly politics of trade policy is in James Bovard's *The Fair Trade Fraud*, Palgrave Macmillan (1992). He has some amazing examples of absurdity in America's trade policy and a superb catalog of the biases in the Department of Commerce's assessment of dumping. For an intellectual history of trade and trade policy, see Douglas Irwin's *Against the Tide: An Intellectual History of Free Trade*, Princeton University Press (1997).

About the Author

Russell Roberts (roberts@gmu.edu) is Professor of Economics at George Mason University, J. Fish and Lillian F. Smith Distinguished Scholar at George Mason's Mercatus Center, and a research fellow at Stanford University's Hoover Institution.

In addition to *The Choice*, he is the author of *The Invisible Heart: An Economic Romance* (MIT Press, 2001).

Roberts blogs with his colleague Don Boudreaux at Cafe Hayek (http://www.cafehayek.com). He is the features editor and a founding advisory board member of the Library of Economics and Liberty (http://www.econlib.org). His podcasts can be found at EconTalk (http://www.econtalk.org). A teacher's guide to this book along with other writing by Roberts can be found at InvisibleHeart.com (http://www. invisibleheart.com).

Index